I0648806

Hugh Allingham

Captain Cuellar's Adventures in Connacht and Ulster

A.D. 1588

Hugh Allingham

Captain Cuellar's Adventures in Connacht and Ulster
A.D. 1588

ISBN/EAN: 9783337081416

Printed in Europe, USA, Canada, Australia, Japan

Cover: Foto ©ninafisch / pixelio.de

More available books at **www.hansebooks.com**

CAPTAIN CUELLAR'S

ADVENTURES

IN

CONNACHT & ULSTER

A.D. 1588.

A PICTURE OF THE TIMES, DRAWN FROM CONTEMPORARY SOURCES.

By HUGH ALLINGHAM, M.R.I.A.,

Member of the Royal Society of Antiquaries (Ireland);
Author of "Ballyshannon: its History and Antiquities," &c.

TO WHICH IS ADDED

An Introduction and Complete Translation

OF

CAPTAIN CUELLAR'S

Narrative of the Spanish Armada

AND HIS ADVENTURES IN IRELAND.

By ROBERT CRAWFORD, M.A., M.R.I.A., &c.

With Map and Illustrations.

LONDON: ELLIOT STOCK, 62, PATERNOSTER ROW.
1897.

[All Rights Reserved.]

Note.

THE favourable reception which was accorded to the paper entitled "The Spanish Armada in Ulster and Connacht," which appeared in Vol. I., Part III., April, 1895, of *The Ulster Journal of Archæology*, and the continued interest in the subject, which seems rather to increase as the literature becomes more extensive, has induced me to re-write the paper, and add much information I was not possessed of when the first paper was printed. Mr. Crawford's most valuable contribution, which forms the second part of this book, should at least justify the present publication. To Francis Joseph Bigger, M.R.I.A., my best thanks are due for the use of copious notes and references, which have been of material assistance.

HUGH ALLINGHAM.

BALLYSHANNON, *May*, 1897.

CAPTAIN CUELLAR'S

Adventures in Connacht and Ulster,

A.D. 1588.

FIGUREHEAD OF A SPANISH GALLEON
WRECKED AT STREEDAGH, 1588.

(*Now in possession of Simon Cullen, J.P.,
Sligo.*)

THE publication of a work entitled "*La Armada Invincible*" [Madrid, 1885], by Captain Cesareo Fernandez Duro, a Spanish naval officer, has been the means of bringing to light many fresh and interesting particulars relating to this ill-fated venture; and, though the incidents narrated are, as might be expected, viewed from the Spanish standpoint, yet the history is written in a spirit of moderation, and gives evidence of great research.

Amongst the valuable documents which have been collected and printed by Captain Duro, that having for its title " Letter of One who was with the Armada for England, and an Account of the Expedition," is of most lively interest to us, seeing that it presents a graphic picture of the North and North-West of Ireland in 1588, drawn by one who was an actual eye-witness of what he describes.

Before proceeding, it may be well to observe that these adventures have already been dealt with by several writers. The *Nineteenth Century*, September, 1885, contained a valuable and interesting paper, entitled "An Episode of the Armada," by the Earl of Ducie. In *Longman's Magazine* [September, October, and November, 1891] appeared "The Spanish Story of the Armada," by J. A. Froude; and in the Proceedings, Royal Irish Academy, 1893, Professor J. P. O'Reilly contributed a paper, entitled "Remarks on Certain Passages in Captain Cuellar's Narrative."

The present paper has been written with the desire to identify some of the places visited by Cuellar while in Connaught and Ulster. His references to these places are, as might have been expected from a foreigner, in many instances obscure; and in order to correctly trace his wanderings, and identify the spots he visited, an intimate acquaintance with the local topography of the district is essential.

Sometimes the clue afforded by his narrative is so slender, that anyone unfamiliar with the localities intended might easily miss the meaning, and be led to an entirely wrong conclusion. The present writer has had the valuable assistance of R. Crawford, C.E., late Professor of Engineering, T.C.D., an accomplished Spanish scholar—not merely a translator—who possesses a practical acquaintance with the idioms of the language. By this knowledge, Mr. Crawford has been able to elucidate many obscure passages in the Spanish book, which would otherwise have proved stumbling-blocks in the way of a proper understanding of the author's meaning. Mr. Crawford has made a literal translation of the whole of Cuellar's letter, which forms the second part of this book. A careful perusal of Mr. Crawford's introductory remarks, and of his translation, will well repay the reader, and is, in fact, needful for the proper understanding of the subject-matter of these pages.

Before entering on Cuellar's adventures on Irish soil, it may be as well to refer to an evident error into which Mr. Froude has fallen in his description of the wreck of the three vessels in Sligo Bay, in one of which Cuellar was. In the article before referred to, the following passage occurs : " Don Martin, after an ineffectual struggle to double Achill Island, had fallen back into the bay, and had anchored off Ballyshannon in a heavy sea with two other galleons. There they lay for four days, from the first to the fifth of September, when, the gale rising, their cables parted, and all three drove on shore on a sandy beach among the rocks. Nowhere in the world does the sea break more violently than on that cruel, shelterless strand," etc. Now, the facts disclosed by Cuellar's narrative, and by other contemporary writers, show that these Spanish ships were not at all near to Ballyshannon ; but having been caught in the violent gales which were then raging round the coast, they were disabled, and being at the best of times unwieldy and difficult to steer, they drifted down from the north, and, failing to double Erris Head, were drawn into Sligo Bay, where they anchored about a mile and a half off shore, in the hope of being able to repair damages, and, when the gales subsided, proceed on their homeward voyage.

Don Francisco Cuellar was captain of the *San Pedro*, a galleon of twenty-four guns, which belonged to the squadron of Castile. The account of Cuellar's adventures, as detailed by himself, are related in the letter to which reference has been made. This document was discovered in the archives of the *Academia de la Historia*, in Madrid, where it had lain in oblivion for three centuries. Passing over the first part of the letter, which relates his adventures in the *San Pedro*, which sustained great damage in an engagement with English vessels off the coast of France, being in a leaky and unseaworthy condition, owing to the number of "shot holes," the *San Pedro*, by order of the mate (Cuellar having retired to take some rest after the fight), moved a short distance away from the Admiral's ship, for the purpose of carrying out some repairs to the damaged hull. This action on the part of the *San Pedro* raised the anger of the Admiral, who ordered Cuellar and another officer to be hanged at the yard's arm. Fortunately for Cuellar this unjust sentence was not carried out in his case, chiefly through the friendly offices of the Judge Advocate—Martin de Aranda.

But Cuellar was no longer left in command of the *San Pedro*: he henceforward sailed in the vessel of the Judge Advocate, who was also styled Provost Marshal. Having passed round the north coast of Scotland, the vessel in which Cuellar was, in company with two other ships—all of large tonnage—encountered head winds and rough weather. Passing Tory Island, they were endeavouring to clear Erris Head on the Mayo coast; but the storms increasing, and the sea running high, they were unable to make that point. With shattered spars and torn canvas, and a weight of water in their holds, which the constant working of the pumps could hardly keep under, these vessels in a rough sea were unmanageable, and, drifting downwards, found themselves enbayed off the Sligo coast, where they hoped to find temporary anchorage. In the sailing instructions given by the Duke of Medina to the Spanish vessels on their return home, the following occurs: "The course that is first to be held is to the north-north-east, until you be found under 61 degrees and a half, and then to take great heed lest you fall upon the Island of Ireland, for fear of the harm that may happen unto you upon that coast. Then parting from those islands, and doubling the Cape in 61 ½ degrees, you shall run west-south-west, until you be found under 58 degrees, and from thence to the south-west," etc. These particulars are valuable in showing the direction in which the Spaniards endeavoured to navigate their unwieldy craft. Captain Duro in his book refers to the frequency of the

A Map of the West and North West Coasts of Ireland, the or— iginal in the British Museum Drawn in 1609. From the showing the places connected with the Spanish Armada.

opening of the seams in the old Spanish ships, which defect he attributes to the excessive weight and height of the masts, whose leverage in heavy weather caused a strain on the hulls which necessitated the constant employment of caulkers.

Cuellar says they anchored half a league from the shore, where they remained "four days without being able to make any provision or do anything. On the fifth day there sprang up such a great storm," he says, "on our beam, with a sea up to the heavens, so that the cables could not hold, nor the sails serve us, and we were driven ashore upon a beach covered with very fine sand, shut in on one side and the other by great rocks. Such a thing was never seen; for within the space of an hour all three ships were broken in pieces, so that there did not escape 300 men, and more than 1,000 were drowned, and amongst them many persons of importance—captains, gentlemen, and other officials." Of the three vessels which were wrecked on the Streedagh Strand—(in a map of the coast, made in 1609, the rock, which is still called *Carrig-na-Spaniagh*, is thus marked: "Three Spanish shipps here cast ashore in Anno Domi, 1588")—the name of one was the *San Juan de Sicilia*. She was commanded by Don Diego Enriquez, "the Hunchback."

This officer, as Cuellar relates, came to his death in a sad way. Fearing the very heavy sea that was washing over the deck of his vessel, which was going to pieces on the strand, he ordered out his large boat, a decked one, and, accompanied by the Count of Villa Franca, and two other Portuguese gentlemen, they closed themselves into the hold of the boat, hoping to be washed ashore. Having gone below, and bringing with them sixteen thousand ducats in jewels and crown pieces, they ordered the hatchway to be tightly fastened down, in order to prevent the ingress of water; but just as the boat was leaving the disabled ship, more than seventy men, terror-stricken with the fate that awaited them, wildly jumped on the deck of the boat, hoping thereby to reach the land; but the small craft, unable to bear the great weight above water-line, and having been struck by a wave, toppled over and sank, all on deck being swept away. She afterwards rose to the surface, and was drifted about in different directions, ultimately reaching the shore upside down. Those unfortunates who were below were all killed, with the exception of Don Diego Enriquez, who, after being in such a sad condition for more than twenty-four hours, was found still living when the hold was broken into by the "savages" who were searching for plunder. They took out the dead men, and Don Diego, who only survived a few minutes; and, having secured the plunder—jewels and money—left the dead stripped and naked on the strand, denying them even the rights of Christian burial! Cuellar, though in great extremities, was not unmindful of the kindness he had received from the Judge Advocate, Martin de Aranda. "One touch of nature makes the whole world kin." Cuellar, the deposed captain, and the Judge Advocate, were standing on the same deck, with the horrors of death facing them on all sides. Martin de Aranda, seeing the destruction of all that was dear to him, had little energy left to make any effort to escape; but Cuellar endeavoured to rally his drooping spirits, and made every effort he could to help him, and bring him to shore. Taking a hatchway from the deck of the vessel they were in, Cuellar got it afloat, and succeeded in getting the Judge Advocate on also; but in the act of casting off from the ship, a huge wave engulphed them, and the Judge Advocate, being unable to hold on, was drowned. Cuellar, grievously wounded by being struck by pieces of floating timber, succeeded in keeping his footing on the hatchway, and at length reached the shore, "unable to stand, all covered with blood, and very much injured."*

Fenton, writing to Burleigh (*State Papers*, 1588-9), says: "At my late being in Sligo, I found both by view of eye and credible report that the number of ships and men perished at these coasts was more than was advertised thither by the Lord Deputy and Council, for I numbered in one strand [Streedagh], of less than five miles in length, eleven hundred dead corpses of men which the sea had driven on the shore. Since the time of the advertisement, the country people told me the like was in other places, though not of like numbers; and the Lord Deputy, writing to the Council, says: 'After leaving Sligo, I journeyed towards Bundroys [Bundrowse] and so to Ballyshannon, the uttermost part of Connaught that way, and riding still along the sea-shore, I went to see the bay where some of these ships were wrecked, and where, as I heard not long before, lay twelve or thirteen hundred of the dead bodies. I rode along that strand near two miles (but left behind me a long mile and more), and then turned off that shore; in both which places, they said that had seen it, there lay as great store of timber of wrecked ships as was in that place which myself had viewed, being in my opinion (having small skill or judgment therein) more than would have built *four* of the greatest ships I ever saw, beside mighty great boats, cables, and other cordage answerable

---

* Amongst those drowned at the wrecks on Streedagh were the following Irishmen: Brian Mac-in-Persium, Andrew Mac-in-Persium, and Cormac O'Larit, all of whom had shipped as sailors in the Spanish vessels.

thereto, and such masts, for bigness and length, as in my knowledge I never saw any two that could make the like.' "

The account given by the Lord Deputy of his journey from Sligo to Ballyshannon, though rather obscurely worded, points to the probability of there having been more than one spot on that coast which was a scene of disaster. It is evident that the entire shore from Streedagh to Bundrowse was littered with the wreckage of the Spanish vessels, and it could hardly be expected that all the "flotsam and jetsam" referred to in the report we have quoted would have come from the three vessels described by Cuellar.

To return to the narrative. Cuellar now found himself in a desperate plight; wounded, half-naked, and starving with hunger, he managed to creep into a place of concealment during the remainder of the day; and he says: "At the dawn of day I began to walk little by little, searching for a monastery of monks that I might repair to it as best I could, the which I arrived at with much trouble and toil, and I found it deserted, and the church and images of the Saints burned and completely ruined, and twelve Spaniards hanging within the church by the act of the English Lutherans, who went about searching for us to make an end of all of us who had escaped from the perils of the sea." Some writers on this shipwreck have been unable to explain this reference to a monastery in the vicinity of the sea-shore at Streedagh. No such difficulty, however, exists in identifying the place indicated; for within sight of the strand stood the *Abbey of Staad*, which tradition says was founded by St. Molaise, the patron saint of the neighbouring island of Inismurray. It was then to this monastery that Cuellar repaired, in the expectation of finding there a safe asylum in his dire necessity. He was, however, disappointed; for he found the place deserted, and several of his fellow-countrymen hanging from the iron bars of the windows. The ruins of Staad Abbey, which still remain, are inconsiderable, consisting of portions of the church, which was oblong in form, and measured, internally, 34 feet in length by 14 feet 5 inches in width. There are indications that a much older building once occupied the site of the existing ruin. Outside the walls of the old church it was customary to light beacons for the purpose of signalling with the inhabitants of Inismurray and elsewhere, and this mode of communication by fire-signals was adopted in Ireland from remote times, and its existence amongst us to the present day is an interesting survival of primitive life. Cuellar, sick at heart with the ghastly spectacle in the monastery, betook himself to a road "which lay through a great wood," and after wandering about without being able to procure any food, he turned his face once more to the sea-shore, in the hope of being able to pick up some provisions that might have been washed in from the wrecks. Here he found, stretched on the strand in one spot, more than 400 Spaniards, and amongst them he recognised *Don Enriquez* and another honoured officer. He dug a hole in the sand and buried his two friends. After some time he was joined by two other Spaniards. They met a man who seemed rather friendly towards them. He directed them to take a road which led from the coast to a village, which Cuellar describes as "consisting of some huts of straw." This was probably the village of Grange, a couple of miles distant; and the huts he refers to were the cabins with thatched roofs, still a common feature in the country. From descriptions of these, which are given by writers of the 16th century, there seems to be but slight difference in the mode of constructing cabins then and now. At Grange was a castle in which soldiers were stationed. It was an important outpost at the period, being on the highway between Connacht and Tirconnell. From this castle, bodies of soldiers used to sally forth, scouring the neighbourhood for Spanish fugitives and plunder. Fearing these military scouts, Cuellar turned off from the village, and entered a wood, in which he had not gone far when a new misfortune befel him. He was set upon by an "old savage," more than seventy years of age, and by two young men—one English, the other French. They wounded him in the leg, and stripped him of what little clothing was left to him. They took from him a gold chain of the value of a thousand reals; also forty-five gold crown pieces he had sewed into his clothing, and some relics that had been given him at Lisbon. But for the interference of a young girl, whom Cuellar describes as of the age of twenty, "and most beautiful in the extreme," it would have gone hard with him in the hands of these men. Having robbed him of all he had, they went on their way in search of further prey, and the young girl, pitying the sad condition of the Spaniard, made a salve of herbs for his wounds, and gave him butter and milk, with oaten bread to eat.

Cuellar was directed to travel in the direction of some mountains, which appeared to be about six leagues distant, behind which there were good lands belonging to an "important savage," a very great friend of the King of Spain. The distances in leagues and miles given in the narrative are in most cases considerably over-estimated, and cannot be relied on. Cuellar, it should be remembered, is describing events which happened to him in a strange country, wherein the names of the places, and the distances from place to place, were alike unknown to him ; and the journeys he was forced to make, in his lame and wretched condition, must have seemed to him very much longer than they were in reality. A right understanding of this part of the narrative is important, as some writers have fallen into the error of supposing that Cuellar's course was in the direction of the *Donegal* Mountains, on the other side of the bay, visible, no doubt, from the locality of the wreck, but on the distant northern horizon. A careful reading of the text will show that this was not the direction he took. He says : "I began to walk as best I could, making for the north* of the mountains, as the boy had told me." This means that he kept on the *north*, or sea-side of the *Dartry* Mountains ; and behind them (*i.e.*, on the *south* side) were good lands belonging to a friendly chief. The word "north" does not here refer to the cardinal point, but is used merely as a relative term, just as "right and left," "back and front," are used in familiar conversation. Besides, Cuellar plainly states the name of the chief he was seeking to reach : he speaks of him as "Senior de Ruerque" (Spanish for *O'Rourque*), whose territory lay in the direction of the mountain range he was travelling towards. He calls him an "important savage"—a term which he applies to the Irish natives he met with, whether friendly or the reverse : it does not refer to their treatment of him personally ; but he intends it to define what he considers their position in the scale of civilization as compared with his own country. Journeying on in the direction pointed out to him, he came to a lake, in the vicinity of which were about thirty huts—all forsaken and untenanted. Going into one of these for shelter, he discovered three other naked men—Spaniards—who had met the same hard treatment as himself. The only food they could obtain here was blackberries and water-cresses. Covering themselves up with some straw, they passed the night in a hut by the lake-side, resolving at daybreak to push forward towards O'Rourke's village.

The lake to which reference is here made is evidently Glenade Lough, from which it was an easy journey to O'Rourke's settlement at Glencar. O'Rourke had another "town" at *Newtown*, on the borders of the County of Sligo. It seems probable, however, that at this time he had removed his people to Glencar. In the Lough here were several crannogs, remains of which are still visible. Such lacustrine habitations were usually resorted to by the Irish chiefs in times of

---

* See Translator's Preface for the sense in which the word "north" is used in Spanish.

disturbance; for within their stockaded lake-dwellings they and their possessions were safest from the attack of the enemy. Having arrived at "the village," Cuellar found the chief absent, being at war with the English, who were at the time in occupation of Sligo. Here he found a number of Spaniards. Before many days passed, tidings came that a Spanish ship, probably one of De Leyva's vessels, was standing off the coast, and on the look-out for any Spaniards who had escaped with their lives. Hearing this, Cuellar and nineteen others resolved to make an effort to reach the vessel. They, therefore, set off at once towards the coast. They met with many hindrances on the way; and Cuellar, probably owing to the wounded state of his leg, was unable to keep pace with the others, and was consequently left behind, while the others got on board the vessel. He regards this circumstance of his being left behind as a special interference of Providence on his behalf, for the ship, after setting sail, was, he says, "wrecked off the same coast, and more than 200 persons were drowned."

Resuming the course of Cuellar's fortunes, we find him pursuing his way by the most secluded routes for fear of the "Sassana horse-men," as he styles the English soldiers. He soon fell in with a clergyman, who entered into friendly converse with him in the Latin tongue—a language, it may be observed, that did not at that period in Ireland rank as a "dead" one—men and women of various degrees, both high and low, spoke it freely; of this there is abundant evidence from contemporary writers. The clergyman gave Cuellar some of the food he had with him, and directed him to take a road which would bring him to a castle which belonged to a "savage" gentleman, "a very brave soldier, and a great enemy of the Queen of England—a man who had never cared to obey her or pay tribute, attending only to his castle and mountains, which [latter] made it strong." Following the course pointed out to him, Cuellar met with an untoward circumstance which caused him much anxiety; he was met by a blacksmith who pursued his calling in a "deserted valley." Here he was forced to abide, and work in the forge. For more than a week he (the Spanish officer) had to blow the forge bellows, and, what was worse, submit to the rough words of the blacksmith's wife, whom he calls "an accursed old woman." At length, his friend the clergyman happened again to pass that way, and seeing Cuellar labouring in the forge, he was displeased. He comforted him, assuring him he would speak to the chief of the castle to which he had directed him, and ask that an escort should be sent for him. The following day this promise was fulfilled, and four men from the castle, and a Spanish soldier who had already found his way thither, arrived, and safely conducted him on his way. Here he seems at last to have found kind and humane treatment. He specially mentions the extreme kindness shown him by the chief's wife, whom he describes as "beautiful in the extreme."

Cuellar, in taking the course pointed out to him by the clergyman, was travelling in an eastward direction, having his back turned on O'Rourke's village, whither he had first gone for succour. The "deserted valley," in which he fell in with the blacksmith, was doubtless the beautiful valley of Glenade, from which place to the island castle of Rossclogher was an easy journey. As this castle is a prominent feature in our narrative, some particulars regarding it and its chiefs may be here noted.

The castle of Rossclogher, the picturesque ruins of which are still prominent in the beautiful scenery of Lough Melvin, was built by one of the clan, at a period—precise date not known—anterior to the reign of Henry VIII. In the *Irish Annals* the name of MacClancy, chief of Dartraigh, appears at A.D. 1241. The territory was held by the family for three hundred years, their property having been finally confiscated after the wars of 1641. The castle lies close to the southern shore of Lough Melvin, considerably to the westward of the island of Inisheher (see Ordnance Map). It is a peculiar structure, being built on an artificial foundation, somewhat similar to the "Hag's Castle" in Lough Mask, and to Cloughoughter Castle in the neighbouring county of Cavan. Here may be noted a striking instance of the accuracy and appropriateness of Irish names of places. When the island of Inisheher (Inis Siar), *i.e.*, western island, got its name, the site of Rossclogher Castle had not been laid, for where the castle stands is considerably further west than the last natural island, which, from its name, marks it as the most westerly island of the lough.

The Irish name of this family was *MacFhlnncdaha*, the name being variously written in the *State Papers* as McGlannogh, McGlanthie, etc., while in the Spanish narrative it is *Manglana*. In a map drawn in 1609, the territory is marked "Dartrie MacGlannagh" (which see). The MacClancys were chiefs, subject to O'Rourke, and their territory—a formidable one, by reason of its mountains and fastnesses—comprised the entire of the present barony of Rossclogher. According to local tradition, which survived when O'Donovan visited the district in the summer of 1836[*], the extent of "Dartree MacClancy" was from *Glack* townland on the east to *Bunduff*

---

on the west—a distance of about six miles ; and from *Mullinaleck* townland on the north to *Aghanlish* on the south—a distance of about
three miles. The townlands of Rossfriar (Ross-na-mbraher, *i.e.*, the
Peninsula of the Friars), and that now called Aghanlish, were ancient
termon lands appertaining to the church of Rossclogher, the ruins of
which stand on the mainland, close to the island castle of our narrative. The romantic and beautiful district over which the
MacClancys held sway included *Lough Melvin*, with its islands
and the mountain range behind. Within its bounds were two
castles—that of Rossclogher and *Dun Carbery*. On the island of
Iniskeen was MacClancy's crannog ; and here it may be pointed out
a frequent error has been made in supposing that the Castle of Rossclogher stood on Iniskeen. The crannog was on that large island
which is far to the east of the Castle of Rossclogher. This was merely
used in troublous times as a place of security—a sort of treasure-
house ; but not an ordinary dwelling-place. Besides the buildings
already mentioned within the territory, were at least three monasteries—that of Doire-Melle, Cacair-Sinchill, and Beallach-in-
Mithidheim—as well as numerous churches, the ruins of some
being still in existence. The MacClancy clan appear to have
sprung from a stock totally distinct from the neighbouring clans
of Brefney. Their chief residence was at Rossclogher, but they had
another castle—that of Dun Carbery—some ruins of which are still
standing close to the village of Tullaghan. This was built in the
sixteenth century, and a more commanding site for a fortified house
it would have been difficult to select. It was built on the summit of
an extensive *Dun*, or fort, which belonged to a period long anterior
to the MacClancy rule ; and it is a noticeable fact that the name of
the original owner of the *Dun Carbery*, son of Niall of the Nine
Hostages (fifth century), has continued to the present day as the
name by which the castle is known.

The Castle of Rossclogher is built on a foundation of heavy stones
laid in the bed of the lake, and filled in with smaller stones and earth
to above water-level. The sub-structure was circular in form, and the
entire was encompassed by a thick wall, probably never more than five
feet in height. The walls of the castle are very thick, and composed
of freestone, obtained from an adjacent quarry on the mainland.
They are cemented together with the usual grouting of lime and coarse
gravel, so generally used by the builders of old ; the outside walls were
coated with thick rough-cast, a feature not generally seen in old
structures in the locality. Facing the south shore, which is about one

hundred yards distant, are the remains of a bastion pierced for musketry. The water between the castle and the shore is deep, and goes down sheer from the foundation.

On the shore, close to the castle, are the remains of military earthworks, evidently constructed by some enemy seeking possession of the castle. On the summit of a hill immediately over this, is a circular enclosure about 220 feet in circumference; it is composed of earth, faced with stone-work. Here the MacClancy-clan folded their flocks and herds, and from this ancient "cattle-booley" a bridle-path led to the mountains above. Portions of this pathway have recently been discovered; it was only two feet in width, and regularly paved with stones enclosed by a kerb.

On the mainland, close to the southern shore, and within speaking distance of the castle, stand the ruins of the old church which was built by MacClancy, and which is of about the same date as the castle to which it was an appendage. In the immediate neighbourhood of the shore, guarded on one side by the lofty mountain range of Dartraigh, on the other by the waters of Lough Melvin, was MacClancy's "town"—an assemblage of primitive huts, probably circular in shape, and of the simplest construction, where dwelt the followers and dependents of the chief, ready, by night or by day, to obey the call to arms, or, as Cuellar expresses it, "Go Santiago," a slang expression in Spain, meaning to attack.*

Of the manners and customs of the natives, Cuellar makes sundry observations. Having described at length how he occupied his leisure in the castle by telling the fortunes of the ladies by palmistry, he mentions incidentally that their conversation was carried on in Latin. He goes on to speak of the natives, or "savages," as he calls them. He says: "Their custom is to live as the brute beasts among the mountains, which are very rugged in that part of Ireland where we lost ourselves. They live in huts made of straw; the men are all large bodied and of handsome features and limbs, active as the roe-deer. They do not eat oftener than once a day, and this is at night; and that which they usually eat is butter with oaten bread. They drink sour milk, for they have no other drink; they don't drink water, although it is the best in the world. On feast days they eat some flesh, half-cooked, without bread or salt, for that is their custom. They clothe themselves, according to their habit, with tight trousers and short loose coats of very coarse goat's hair. They cover them-

---

* *Santiago,* the Patron Saint of Spain: hence it became the war-cry or watchword when going to battle.

selves with blankets, and wear their hair down to their eyes. They are great walkers, and inured to toil. They carry on perpetual war with the English, who here keep garrison for the Queen, from whom they defend themselves, and do not let them enter their territory, which is subject to inundation and marshy."

The reference Cuellar makes to the food of the Irish with whom he sojourned is interesting. He says: "They do not eat oftener than once a day, and this is at night, and that which they usually eat is butter with *oaten bread*." The partiality for oaten bread here spoken of still survives; but its use has within the last half century greatly declined, owing to the extensive introduction of "white bread," the term applied to ordinary bakers' loaves. When the tide of emigration to America—in the early part of this century—was in full flow from Ballyshannon, the emigrants had to provide their own food on the voyage from this port to the Western Continent, and that universally taken with them was an ample supply of oaten cakes. It may not be out of place here to refer to the curious belief which still lives in the minds of the peasantry of this district, though, like most of the survivals of folk-lore, it is fading from the memories of the people.

The *Feàr-Gortha*, or Hungry Grass, is believed to grow in certain spots, and whoever has the bad luck to tread on this baneful fairy herb is liable to be stricken down with the mysterious complaint. The symptoms, which come on suddenly, are complete prostration, preceded by a general feeling of weakness; the sufferer sinks down, and, if assistance is not at hand, he perishes. It is believed that if food be partaken of in the open air, and the fragments remaining be not thrown as an offering to the "good folk," that they will mark their displeasure by causing a crop of "hungry grass" to arise on the spot and produce the effects described. Fortunately, the cure is as simple as the malady is mysterious. *Oatcake* is the specific, or, in its absence, a few grains of oatmeal. The wary traveller who knows the dangers of the road, carries in his pocket a small piece of oatcake, not intended as food, but as a charm against the *Feàr-Gortha*.

Cuellar also observes that the chief inclination of these people is to plunder their neighbours, capturing cattle and any other property obtainable, the raids being chiefly carried out at night. He also remarks that the English garrison were in the habit of making plundering expeditions into the territory of these natives, and the only refuge they had was, on the approach of the soldiers, to withdraw to the mountains with their families and cattle till the danger would be past. Speaking of the women, he says: "Most of them are very beautiful, but badly-dressed. The head-dress of the women is a linen cloth, doubled over the head and tied in front." He remarks "the women are great workers and housekeepers, after their fashion." Speaking of the churches, etc., he says most of them have been demolished by the hands of the English, and by those natives who have joined them, who are as bad as they. He concludes his by-no-means flattering description in these words: "In this kingdom there is neither justice nor right, and everyone does what he pleases."

The "sour milk" Cuellar speaks of is buttermilk, as great a favourite here in the nineteenth century as in the sixteenth. The cloth which he calls "very coarse goats' hair" was probably the familiar homespun woollen frieze, which from the earliest times was made by the Irish. The head-dress of the women—a linen cloth—is still adopted by elderly women here.

After enjoying a short period of rest in MacClancy's, or, as Cuellar styles it, Manglana's castle, rumours of an alarming nature reached them. The Lord Deputy Fitzwilliam, or, as he is called in the narrative, "the great governor of the Queen," was marching from Dublin, with a force of 1,700 soldiers, in search of the lost ships and the people who had escaped the fury of the waves, and no quarter could be expected for either the Irish chiefs or the shipwrecked Spaniards; all that came within Fitzwilliam's grasp would certainly be hanged. Cuellar says the Lord Deputy marched along the whole coast till he arrived at the place where the shipwreck happened (at Streedagh), and from thence he came towards the castle of "Manglana." It is at this point of his narrative that he first mentions the name of the chief who had given him refuge.

MacClancy seeing the force that had come against him, felt him-self unable to stand a siege, and decided to escape to the friendly shelter of his mountains. He called Cuellar aside and made known his determination, and advised that he and the other Spaniards should consider what they would do for their own safety. Cuellar consulted with his fellows, and they finally agreed that their only chance of life was to hold out in the castle as long as possible, trusting to its strength and isolated situation; and, leaving the result to the fortunes of war, they determined to stand or fall together.

Having communicated their decision to MacClancy, he willingly provided them with all the arms within his reach, and a sufficient store of provisions to last for six months. He made them take an oath to hold the castle "till death," and not to open the gates for

" Irishman, Spaniard, or anyone else till his return." Having made these preparations, and removed the furniture and relics out of the church on the shore, and deposited them within the castle, MacClancy, after embracing Cuellar, withdrew to the mountains, taking with him his family and followers, with their flocks and herds. Cuellar now provided himself with several boat-loads of stones, six muskets, and six crowbars, as well as a supply of ammunition. He gives a minute description of the place he was going to defend. He says : " The castle is very strong and very difficult to take, if they do not attack it with artillery, for it is founded in a lake of very deep water, which is more than a league wide at some parts, and three or four leagues long, and has an outlet to the sea ; and besides, with the rise of spring tides, it is not possible to enter it ; for which reason the castle could not be taken by water, nor by the shore of land which is nearest it, neither could injury be done it, because a league around the 'town,' which is established on the mainland, it is marshy, breast deep, so that even the inhabitants [natives] could not get to it except by paths." These paths, through bogs and shallow lakes, were made of large stones in a hidden, irregular way, unknown to any except those who had the key to their position. Three centuries ago, the aspect of the country was very different from what it now is : the land was in a swampy, undrained condition, and, beyond small patches here and there, which had been cleared for growing corn, dense thickets of brushwood covered the surface everywhere; and, as there were no roads or bridges, but merely narrow paths, where two horsemen could not pass each other, the difficulty—not to say impossibility—of bringing troops, heavy baggage, and artillery across country is apparent. That such a state of things existed in MacClancy's territory there is abundant evidence. The stones with which Cuellar provided himself were a favourite item in the war materials of that period : these were used with deadly effect from the towers of castles, and were also thrown from cannon instead of iron balls. Cuellar says : " Our courage seemed good to the whole country, and the enemy was very indignant at it, and came upon the castle with his forces—about 1,800 men—and observed us from a distance of a mile and a half from it, without being able to approach closer on account of the water [or marshy ground] which intervened." From this description, it is evident the Lord Deputy's forces had taken up their position on the shore of the opposite promontory of Rossfriar—a tongue of land which projects itself into the lough at the north-west end. From this point he says they exhibited "menaces and warnings," and hanged two

Spanish fugitives they had laid hold of, "to put the defenders in fear." The troops demanded by trumpet a surrender of the castle, but the Spaniards declined all proposals. For seventeen days, Cuellar says, the besiegers lay against them, but were unable to get a favourable position for attack. "At length, a severe storm and a great fall of snow compelled them to withdraw without having accomplished anything." In the *State Papers*, under date 12th October, 1588, the Lord Deputy asks the Privy Council of England to send at once two thousand "sufficient and thoroughly appointed men" to join

THE SPANIARDS HOLDING ROSSCLOGHER CASTLE AGAINST THE LORD DEPUTY.

the service directed against the main body of 3,000 Spaniards in O'Donnell's country and the North. In the same month, Fenton writes to the Lord Deputy "that the Spaniards are marching towards Sligo, and are very near Lough Erne." There were, no doubt, a large number of Spaniards who had escaped the dangers of the sea, and had fled for refuge to O'Donnell, O'Neill, and O'Rourke, all of whom were very favourable to them; but the Lord Deputy, for his own ends, greatly exaggerated both their numbers and strength. They were merely fugitives acting on the defensive, and not then inclined to be aggressive. They well knew the fate of hundreds of their countrymen, and what they might expect if they fell into the hands of the Lord Deputy.

In the County of Clare, at this time, was another MacClancy—Boethius. He was Elizabeth's High Sheriff there, and, unlike his namesake of Rossclogher, he cruelly treated and killed a number of Spaniards of the Armada, who had been shipwrecked off that coast. In memory of his conduct then, he is cursed every seventh year in a church in Spain. In the *State Papers* no reference is made to this expedition against MacClancy's castle; all that is said is that troops arrived at Athlone on 10th November, 1588, and returned to Dublin on 23rd December following, "without loss of any one of her Majesty's army; neither brought I home, as the captains inform me, scarce twenty sick persons or thereabouts; neither found I the water, nor other great impediments which were objected before my going out, to have been dangerous, otherwise than very reasonable to pass." In these vague terms Fitzwilliam disposes of a disagreeable subject which he knew was more for his own credit not to enlarge upon. It seems probable that Cuellar has over-estimated the number of soldiers sent to storm the castle which he was defending; there is, however, no ground for doubting the general truth of his account of the transaction. MacClancy, we know, was the subject of peculiar hatred by the authorities; Bingham describes him as "an arch-rebel, and the most barbarous creature in Ireland," and the fact of his having given shelter to Spanish fugitives made him ten times worse in their eyes.

Fitzwilliam, the Lord Deputy, whom Cuellar styles the "Great Governor," was a covetous and merciless man. Not long after his arrival in Ireland, the Spanish shipwrecks took place, and the rumours of the great amount of treasure and valuables which the Spaniards were reported to have with them called into prominence the most marked feature in the Lord Deputy's character—cupidity. His commission shows this : "To make by all good means, both of oaths and *otherwise* [this means *by torture*], to take all hulls of ships, treasures, etc., into your hands, and to apprehend and execute all Spaniards of what quality soever . . . . torture may be used in prosecuting this enquiry."

In the *State Papers*, at December 3, 1588—Sir R. Bingham to the Queen—the following reference to the Lord Deputy's expedition to the North of Ireland is made: "But the Lord Deputy, having further advertisements from the North of the state of things in those parts, took occasion to make a journey thither, and made his way through this province [Connaught], and in passing along caused both these two Spaniards, which my brother [George Bingham] had, to be executed." One of these was Don Graveillo de Swasso. At December 31st, the Lord Deputy thus refers to his movements : "At my coming to the Castles of Ballyshannon and Beleek, which stand upon the river Earne, and are in possession of one Sir Owen O'Toole, *alias* O'Gallagher*, a principal man of that country, I found all the country [people] and cattle fled into the strong mountains and fastnesses of the woods in their own countrie and neighbours adjoining, as O'Rourke, O'Hara, the O'Glannaghies [MacClancy], Maguires, and others." In the *State Papers*, 15th October, 1588, we learn some curious particulars concerning the wreck of one of the Spanish ships, named *La Trinidad Valencera*, at Inisowen (O'Doherty's country). This vessel, which was a very large one (1,100 tons), carried 42 guns and 360 men, including soldiers and mariners, many of whom were drowned. They had only one boat left, and this a broken one, in which they succeeded in landing a part of the crew. Some swam to shore, and the rest were landed in a boat they bought from the Inisowen men for 200 ducats. Some curious details are given of how the Spaniards fared on land. When first they came ashore, with only their rapiers in their hands, they found four or five "savages," who bade them welcome, and well-used them : afterwards, some twenty more "wild men" came to them, and robbed them of a money-bag containing 1,000 reals of plate and some rich apparel. The only food they could obtain was horse-flesh, which they bought from the country people, as well as a small quantity of butter. When they had been about a week living here, Fitzwilliam's men came on the scene, as also O'Donnell and his wife. The Spaniards surrendered to the captains that carried "the Queen's ensigns," the conditions being that their lives should be spared till they appeared before the Lord Deputy, and be allowed to take with them a change of apparel from the stores of their own ship. These conditions were not adhered to, and the soldiers and natives were allowed to spoil and plunder the shipwrecked Spaniards. The O'Donnell above referred to was the father of the celebrated Red Hugh, who was at this period within the walls of Dublin Castle, a close prisoner. "O'Donnell's wife" was the celebrated Ineen Dubh, the mother of Red Hugh. O'Donnell felt himself weak and unable to cope with the English power, which was surrounding him on all sides. While not taking an active part in

---

* Sir Owen O'Gallagher was O'Donnell's Marshal, and lived in the Castle of Ballyshannon at this period.

maltreating the Spaniards, who had been thrown on his territory by the violence of the storms, he was guilty in a passive way of permitting them to be ill-used; and when, a short time after these events, he resigned the government of Tirconnell to the more capable hands of his son, Red Hugh, and retired to the solitude of the cloister, the greatest sin which weighed on his conscience was his cruel conduct in slaying a number of Spanish seamen in Inisowen, which act was instigated by the Lord Deputy.

MacClancy at length paid dearly for his part in the Spanish affair. This we learn from a letter in the *State Papers*, under date 23rd April, 1590: "The acceptable service performed by Sir George Bingham in cutting off M'Glanaghie, an arch-rebel . . . M'Glanaghie's head brought in. M'Glanaghie ran for a lough, and tried to save himself by swimming, but a shot broke his arm, and a gallowglass brought him ashore. He was the most barbarous creature in Ireland; his countrie extended from Grange till you come to Ballishannon; he was O'Rourke's right hand; he had fourteen Spaniards with him, some of whom were taken alive." The lough above referred to is Lough Melvin. MacClancy was endeavouring to reach his fortress when he met his end. O'Rourke, shortly after these events, fled to Scotland, where he was arrested, brought to London, arraigned on a charge of high treason, found guilty, and hanged. At the place of execution he was met by the notorious *Myler M'Grath*, that many-sided ecclesiastic, whose castle walls, near Pettigo, still keep his name in remembrance. M'Grath endeavoured to make him abjure his faith, but O'Rourke could not be shaken; he knew the sordid character of the man, and bitterly reproached him for his own mercenary conduct.

When the siege was raised, MacClancy and his followers returned from the mountains, and made much of Cuellar and his comrades, asking them to remain and throw in their lot with them. To Cuellar he offered his sister in marriage. This, however, the latter declined, saying he was anxious to turn his face homewards. MacClancy would not hear of the Spaniards leaving; and Cuellar, fearing he might be detained against his will, determined to leave unobserved, which he did two days after Christmas, when he and four Spanish soldiers left the castle before dawn, and went "travelling by the mountains and desolate places," and at the end of twenty days they came to *Dunluce*, where Alonzo de Leyva, and the Count de Paredes, and many other Spanish nobles had been lost; and there, he says, "they went to the huts of some 'savages,' who told us of the great misfortunes of our people who were drowned."

Cuellar does not indicate the course he took in travelling on foot from the castle in Lough Melvin to Dunluce; but it is evident, from the time spent on the journey, that it was the circuitous route round the coast of Donegal to Derry, and from thence to Dunluce. Their journey was one of danger, as military scouts were searching the country everywhere for Spaniards, and more than once he had narrow escapes. After some delay and considerable difficulty, Cuellar, through the friendly assistance of Sir James MacDonnell, of Dunluce, succeeded in crossing over to Scotland, in company with seventeen Spanish sailors who had been rescued by MacDonnell. He hoped to enjoy the protection of King James VI., who was then reported to favour the Spaniards.

Cuellar did not find things much better there, and, after some delay, he eventually took ship and arrived at Antwerp. His narrative is dated October 4, 1589, and was evidently not written till his arrival on the Continent. In forming an estimate of its value, it should be remembered that the greater part, if not all, was written by him from memory. It is highly improbable he would have made notes, or kept a diary in Ireland, as the writing of his adventures never occurred to him (as his narrative shows) till afterwards. This most probable supposition will account for any inaccuracies in his statements as to places, distances, etc.; and allowing for a natural tendency to exaggeration, Cuellar's narrative, corroborated as it is in all essential points by contemporary history, bears on its face the stamp of truth and authenticity.

The *State Papers* (Ireland) at this year [1588] contain several references to these wrecks on the Connaught coast.* Amongst them the following occur : "After the Spanish fleet had doubled Scotland, and were in their course homewards, they were by contrary weather driven upon the several parts of this province [Connaught] and wrecked, as it were, by even portions—three ships in every of the four several counties bordering on the sea coasts, viz., in Sligo, Mayo, Galway, and Thomond :—so that twelve ships perished on the rocks and sands of the shore-side, and some three or four besides to seaboard of the out-isles, which presently sunk, both men and ships, in the night-time. And so can I say by good estimation that six or seven thousand men have been cast away on these coasts, save some 1,000 of them which escaped to land in several places where their ships fell, which sithence *were all put to the sword.*" Of all the ships

---

* Sir R. Bingham to Walsyngham, Oct. 1st, 1588.

which composed the Armada, none was a greater object of interest than the *Rata*, a great galleon commanded by Don Alonzo de Leyva. This officer was Knight of Santiago and Commendador of Alcuesca : a remarkable man, of invincible courage and perseverance, who was destined to meet a watery grave on this expedition. It is said that King Philip felt more grief for his death than for the loss of the whole fleet.

In the *Rata* were hundreds of youths of the noblest families of Castile, who had been committed to De Leyva's care. Having cleared the northern coast of Scotland and gained the Atlantic, he kept well out to sea, and in the early part of the month of September doubled Erris Head, on the western coast of Mayo, after which he and another galleon came to anchor in Blacksod Bay. Here he sent in a boat, with fourteen men, to ascertain the disposition of the natives, whether friendly or the reverse. Having landed, they soon encountered one of the petty chiefs—Richard Burke by name, familiarly known as the "Devil's Son." This man, true to his character, robbed and maltreated them. Immediately after this a violent storm sprang up, which proved fatal to many of the Spanish ships then off the Irish coast : the *Rata* broke loose from her anchors, and ran ashore ; De Leyva and his men were only able to escape with their lives, carrying with them their arms and any valuables they could lay hold of. They set fire to the *Rata*; and perceiving hard by an old castle, within it they took up their quarters. The "Devil's Son" and his followers made their way to the wreck, plundering any of the rich garments and stores which they could snatch from the flames. At this juncture, *Bryan-na-Murtha O'Rourke*, Prince of Breffney, hearing of the abject condition of the Spaniards, sent them immediate assistance, and an invitation to their commander, De Leyva, to come to his castle at Dromahair. There they were well entertained, comfortably clothed, and provided with arms. This is referred to in the Irish *State Papers* thus : "Certain Spaniards being stript were relieved by Sir Brian O'Rourke, apparelled, and new furnished with weapons."

O'Rourke, whose power and popularity were very great, was a dangerous foe to the Governor of Connaught, who was unable to make him pay the "Queen's Rent." His action in harbouring and succouring the Spaniards, and for a short space enlisting them in his service, had, as shall be seen further on, important results in his approaching downfall. De Leyva resolved, after some time, to quit the country, and to embark his men in the other galleon, the *San Martin*, which had been able to hold out in the offing. Having made sail, and on their way fallen in with the *Girona* and another ship—a galliass—they endeavoured to clear *Rossan* Point; but the sea being still very rough and the wind unpropitious, they were obliged to make for Killybegs. Having reached the entrance to that port, the two larger vessels went on the rocks, and became wrecks; the galliass continued to float, though badly injured; the crews and soldiers, numbering two thousand, were got ashore with their arms, but no provisions were saved.

The *State Papers* [September, 1588] say that "John Festigan, who came out of the barony of Carbric [of which Streedagh strand forms a part], saw *three great ships* coming from the south-west, and bearing towards O'Donnell's country, and took their course right to the harbour of Killybegs, the next haven to Donegal." And in the examination of a Spanish sailor named Macharg,* the following reference appears: "After the fight in the narrow sea, she fell upon the coast of Ireland in a haven called 'Erris St. Donnell,' where, at their coming in, they found a great ship called the *Rata*, of 1,000 tons or more, in which was Don Alonzo de Leyva. After she perished, Don Alonzo and all his company were received into the hulk of *St. Anna*, with all the goods they had in the ships of any value; as plate, apparel, money, jewels, and armour, leaving behind them victual, ordnance, and much other stuff, which the hulk was not able to carry away." It will be seen from the above that it is stated that it was in the *St. Anna* De Leyva embarked, after the loss of his own vessel; but it would appear from "*La Felicissima Armada*" that it was in the *San Martin* they took ship, and afterward removed to the *Duquesa Santa Anna*.

The number of wrecks of the Spanish vessels on the Irish coast was largely due to the insufficiency of their anchor-gear; and in explanation of this, it may be observed that it was chiefly *hempen* cables which were then in use; and even in the largest vessels substantial chain cables had not been adopted.

It would seem that when De Leyva had reached "O'Donnell's country," he found the *San Martin* so much injured and in such a leaky condition, that he abandoned her and placed his men and valuables in the *Duquesa Santa Anna*, which, through the friendly aid of O'Neill and McSwine, he was enabled to repair. After obtaining fresh stores of provisions from the people of Tirconnell, De Leyva once more put to sea; but misfortune still followed in his track, and the *Santa Anna*

---

* Duro, p. 98; 25, i.

ran on the rocks in Glennageveny Bay, a few miles west of Inisowen
Head. Still undaunted, De Leyva, though now sorely wounded in
escaping from the wreck, made another effort. The *Girona*, which
had also been patched up while at Killybegs, lay at anchor in a creek
in McSwine's territory, about twenty miles distant from where he now
was. In the *Girona* he determined to sail, and being unable to walk
or ride had himself carried across country, the remnant of his men
following him—for many had been drowned. Close to the shore, in
sight of that relentless sea from which they had already suffered
so keenly, these belated men encamped for the space of a week, using
every effort to make the *Girona*—their last means of escape—as tight

WRECK OF A GALLEON AT PORT-NA-SPANIAGH, NORTH COAST OF ANTRIM, SEPTEMBER, 1588.

and seaworthy as possible. They once more embarked, hoping to be
able at least to reach the coast of Scotland; but their course was
nearly run; and after a few days, while passing near to the Giant's
Causeway, they ran on a rock, and in a few minutes were dashed to
pieces. It is said every soul on board except five sailors—nobles,
mariners, soldiers, and slaves (who were kept as rowers)—were lost.
The actual spot of the wreck pointed to by tradition still bears the
name of "*Spaniard Rock*," the western head of Port-na-Spaniagh.

The *State Papers* (Ireland, 1588) contain the following reference
to this event: "The Spanish ship [the *Girona*] which arrived in

Tirconnell with the McSweeny, was on Friday, the 18th of this present month [*Oct., 1588*], descried over against *Dunluce*, and by rough weather was perished, so that there was driven to the land, being drowned, the number of 260 persons, with certain butts of wine, which Sorely Boy [MacDonnell] hath taken up for his use." There was another of the Spanish ships wrecked near Dunluce, but the name of the vessel is unknown. From this wreck the MacDonnells recovered three pieces of cannon, which were subsequently claimed by Sir John Chichester for the Government. These cannon were mounted on Dunluce Castle, and MacDonnell refused to give them up. He had also rescued eleven sailors from this wreck, as well as the five from the *Girona*. These he all took under his protection, and eventually sent them over in a boat to Scotland, from whence they made their way home. From the depositions of an Irish sailor named *McGrath*, who was on board the *Girona*, it appears that vessel went aground on a long, low reef of rock at the mouth of the *Bush* river, which reef was then known as the "Rock of Bunbois."

Of the authentic relics of the Armada, those which have attracted most attention, and been the subject of most controversy, are the iron chests. That there are a greater number of these chests still preserved in Ireland than could reasonably be assumed to have belonged to the Spanish vessels which perished on the Irish coast, cannot be denied; nevertheless, it is a mistake which some writers on the subject have fallen into, in supposing that no such chests were in the Spanish vessels, and that they are a mere popular fiction, as their introduction into Ireland must have been at least a century later than the Armada period. The writer has been at pains to obtain from the most trustworthy sources, both in this country and in England, all the information possible, and the result is here summarized. Having examined specimens of these treasure-chests in South Kensington and elsewhere, belonging to the 14th, 15th, and 16th centuries, from the earliest chest downwards, the same features are apparent in their construction and ornamentation. They were by no means peculiar to Spain, but were the typical and recognised receptacles for valuables all over the Continent of Europe for many centuries.* In Ireland these chests were in use in the time of the O'Donnells, and were doubtless brought over in the vessels which were frequently trading between the ports of Tirconnell and the Brabant Marts. Within the past half-century, while some clay was

---

* Chests of the same type, called *Arca*, were discovered in the excavations at Pompeii, where they were used for keeping the public money.

being turned up and removed from the precincts of *O'Clery's Castle*, at Kilbarron, near Ballyshannon, the lid of one was discovered with the intricate system of bolts and levers attached. This is now in the custody of the writer, having been kindly lent to him by the owner, General Tredennick, Woodhill, Ardara. When brought to light, it was supposed to have been the lock of the chief entrance to O'Clery's stronghold, and continued to be so regarded till identified by the writer as a portion of a fifteenth-century coffer. This discovery proves beyond question that these chests *were* in use in Ireland, whether

A SPANISH TREASURE-CHEST.

brought over in Spanish or other vessels, at a much earlier date than some have supposed. The lid found at O'Clery's Castle, it is reasonable to infer, belonged to a chest which was used by the historians of Tirconnell for the safe keeping of their valuable manuscripts and other articles; and, looking to the fact that their house and property were confiscated within a period of twenty years or so after the Spanish wrecks, and that Kilbarron was then plundered and dismantled, there can be no doubt that the chest in question belonged to the period when the O'Clerys flourished in their rock-bound fortress. The lid itself offers a curious bit of evidence of its past history: a portion of one of the hinges remains attached, showing that it had been wrenched off with violence, and that the chest to which it belonged had been forced by some plundering enemy who had not possession of the master-key, which actuated all the bolts of the lock. A similar lid was found in the ruins of O'Donnell's Castle at Donegal, and is still in existence in this neighbourhood.

There is in the possession of W. E. Kelly, Esq., St. Helen's, Westport, Co. Mayo (to whom the writer is indebted for the information), a very interesting treasure-chest, which bears satisfactory evidence of having been recovered from one of the Armada ships wrecked on that coast in 1588. After "the flight of the Earls," a branch of the O'Donnells migrated from Tirconnell to *Newport*, Co. Mayo, and one of the family—Conel O'Donnell, brother of Sir Neal O'Donnell—obtained from a peasant, who lived on the sea-shore at Clew Bay, the chest in question. No particulars are forthcoming as to the exact spot where the peasant found it; but it bears evidence, from its corrosion, of having been subjected to the prolonged action of sea water, and it is not unlikely that this relic was on board the *Rata*, which De Leyva set fire to in Blacksod Bay. The size of the chest is 2 ft. 10½ ins. long, 1 ft. 9 ins. wide, and 1 ft. 7½ ins. high.

In the Armada Exhibition, at Drury Lane, held October, 1888, the following amongst other relics were shown :

"No. 240.—Spanish treasure-chest, with two keys; the larger key is emblematical, the bow being the ecclesiastical A.N., the wards being 'chevron' and 'cross.' Inside of chest has engraved face-plate to lock, perforated with *Spanish eagles* for design.

"No. 241.—Spanish treasure-chest, believed to have come out of the *Santa Anna*, etc.

"No. 242.—Iron chest from Armada. This chest is of most remarkable construction : there is an apparent keyhole, but the real one is concealed in the lid, which is one large lock, the lock-plate of which is of very fine workmanship of polished iron.

"No. 243.—Iron treasure-chest, taken from the Spanish war-ship during the fight with the Armada.

"Spanish matchlock, taken from a Spaniard on the coast of Ireland.

"Spear head, from one of the Armada ships, wrecked off the coast of Donegal.

"A spoon of curious floral design, found on the shore close to Dunluce Castle, about 90 years ago [supposed to be from the wreck of the *Girona*.]" *

---

* From the Official Catalogue of Tercentenary Exhibition of Spanish Armada.

Turning to Cuellar's narrative, in speaking of the wrecks at Streedagh, Co. Sligo, of which he was an eye-witness, the following occurs : * "And then [the Irish] betook themselves to the shore to plunder and break open *money chests*." These are called in Spanish *Arcas*, *i.e.*, iron chests with flat lids to hold money, etc.

In the *State Papers* (Ireland, 1588) several references to money chests in the Spanish ships appear. "Plate and ducats" are spoken of as being "rifled out of their chests." At 2nd Aug., 1588 [examination of Spanish prisoners], from the "*Nuestra Señora del Rosario*," "a *chest of the King's* was taken wherein was 52,000 ducats, of which chest Don Pedro de Valdez had one key and the King's treasurer or the Duke another. Besides [it is added], many of the gentlemen had good store of money aboard the said ship; also, there was wrought plate and a great store of precious jewels and rich apparel."

In *State Papers* [4th and 5th August, 1588], in describing the capture of a Spanish "*Carrack*"—the *San Salvador*—it is said: "This very night some inkling came unto us that a *chest* of great weight should be found in the fore-peak of the ship," etc. These and many other references to both treasure and treasure-chests, taken from contemporary sources, show that the Spanish treasure-chests *are not* mythical, but formed a necessary part of the outfit of an expedition, on which those who had entered had staked all their riches and had brought their valuables with them. A fine specimen of the treasure-chest is in the possession of Major Hamilton, Brownhall. It has been in his family for such a period that its history is lost. The ornamental open-work of polished steel, which covers the inside of lid, is a very fine specimen of mediæval iron work.

In Western Tirconnell is a cluster of islands which, collectively, are called *The Rosses*. About four and a half miles north-west of Mullaghderg are the "Spanish Stags" or "Enchanted Ships." On this wild and rocky coast, abounding in shoals and sunken rocks, one of the Spanish ships was cast away. Here lies buried in the sand the remains of one of them. A little more than a century ago, an expedition of young men, whose imagination was heated by the traditional accounts of buried treasure, set out in a boat to the Spanish rock, and being good divers and expert swimmers, they succeeded in reaching the wreck. They got on the upper deck, and were able by great effort and perseverance to recover a quantity of lead : they raised a number of brass guns, some of which were 10 feet

---

* See Mr. Crawford's translation and relative note, Part II.

long. These were broken up and sold as scrap metal at 4½d. per lb. The iron guns, of which they found a number, were left in the water. This vessel, tradition says, was a treasure ship; at all events, a number of Spanish gold coins were found, and were in existence some years ago. The brass cannon which were found bore the Spanish arms. It is said some of the Spaniards from this vessel escaped to land, and spent the rest of their lives amongst the Irish in The Rosses.

In the spring of 1895, an attempt was made to search for the remains of this ship. A small steamer, called the *Harbour Lights*, visited the spot, and remained for a fortnight, but without being able to accomplish anything. Owing to the accumulation of sand, which now covers the wreck, there are great obstacles in the way of reaching it. At about a distance of two miles to the south of the

"Spanish Rock" another vessel was wrecked, in the Bay of Castle-fort, inside of the North Island of Aran. In 1853, the coastguards at Rutland, under the superintendence of their chief officer, Mr. Richard Heard, and at the instance of Admiral Sir Erasmus Ommanney, C.B., who was on a tour of inspection in that year, had their attention directed to the wreck. The search was rewarded by the recovery of a fine anchor, which was forthwith transmitted to London, and presented by the Admiral to the United Service Institution, Whitehall Place. Through the kindness of Sir Erasmus Ommanney, an engraving* of this interesting relic is presented, and the writer is also indebted to

* From a photograph kindly taken by T. B. M'Dowell, Esq., London.

him for the particulars of the discovery of the anchor. A portion of
one of the brass cannon recovered from the *Girona* was in Castle-
caldwell Museum, till the collection was disposed of. The fine
figurehead of one of the ships wrecked off Streedagh, which is shown
on the first page, is the only existing specimen in Ireland. In the
Parish Church of Carndonagh is a bell, which tradition says was
recovered from an Armada vessel wrecked at Inishowen. It bears
the following legend: "Sancta: Maria: Ora: Pro: Nobis Ricardus
Pottar [his sign or trade mark] De Vruain Me Fecit Alla [Allelujah].

The following are the names of the Spanish vessels lost on the
coasts of Ulster and Connacht, so far as they are known (several
nameless vessels were also cast away):

Duquesa Santa Anna	900 tons.
The Rata	820 ,,
The San Martin	—
El Gran Grifon, Capitana	650 ,,
The Girona	—
The San Juan	... 530 ,,
La Trinidad Valencera	... 1,100 ,,

In the valuable work, entitled "State Papers relating to the Defeat
of the Spanish Armada, Anno 1588," by Professor Laughton (Navy
Records Society)—a work which throws much light on the history of
the period, and should be studied in connection with Captain Duro's
book—the following remarks are made as to the cause of the loss of
so many Spanish vessels: "The Spanish ships were lost partly from
bad pilotage, partly from bad seamanship, but chiefly because they
were leaking like sieves, had no anchors, their masts and rigging
shattered, their water casks smashed."

The actual numbers when the fleet sailed from the Tagus
on the 20th May were: 130 ships, 57,868 tons, 2,431 guns, 8,050
seamen, 18,973 soldiers, 1,382 volunteers, 2,088 slaves (as rowers).

PART II.

LIBRARY OF PRINCETON

MAY 7 – 1928

THEOLOGICAL SEMINARY

CAPTAIN CUELLAR'S

NARRATIVE

OF

THE SPANISH ARMADA

AND OF

His Wanderings and Adventures in Ireland.

(Dated October 4th, 1589).

TRANSLATED BY

ROBERT CRAWFORD, M.A., M.R.I.A., &c.,

From the Spanish Text,

AS GIVEN IN

"*LA ARMADA INVENCIBLE,*"

BY CAPTAIN CESAREO FERNANDEZ DURO,

Published in Madrid, 1884-5.

Translator's Preface.

SHORTLY after the publication in Madrid of the second volume of Captain Duro's book—"*La Armada Invencible*"—the Earl of Ducie drew special attention to it in an article which appeared in the number of the *Nineteenth Century* for September, 1885.

Subsequently Mr. Froude took up the subject, and discoursed upon it in *Longman's Magazine* for September, October, and November, 1891, giving a general sketch of the salient features of the ill-fated expedition from the Spanish point of view, as disclosed in the pages of the book in question.

These glowing pictures aroused much public interest at the time ; but they were especially attractive to those persons who happened to combine the conditions of possessing antiquarian tastes, and living near the localities brought into prominence by the recital of the great disasters which befel the "Invincible Armada."

Of all the exciting scenes in that eventful episode in our history, none was more tragic than the wreck of three of the largest of the Spanish ships, which took place, simultaneously, in the bay of Donegal, on the north-west coast of Ireland, in September, 1588.

The fact that in Captain Duro's book there appeared a hitherto unpublished narrative of the event, written at the time by Don Francisco Cuellar, one of the survivors of the catastrophe, and giving a minute account of his wanderings and adventures in the country where he was cast away, contributed to increase the local interest in the matter.

Mr. Hugh Allingham at once began a series of exhaustive investigations in relation to Cuellar's descriptions, the results of which he subsequently placed before the public in the pages of the *Ulster Journal of Archæology*, April, 1895.

It was solely with the object of assisting him in the researches he then undertook that this translation was prepared, and there was no intention at the time of any future publication of it.

It was a matter of importance to facilitate the process of identification as regards the various localities referred to, as well as to avoid the danger of misinterpreting the writer's meaning when dealing with obscure passages ; conditions requiring the translation to be as literal as possible, and leaving the translator with but little freedom in treating a language that at best does not lend itself easily to reproduction in the English idiom.

These facts are mentioned to account for the style in which it has been prepared, as it has no pretensions to merit, except in so far as care has been taken to follow closely the wording of the original Spanish.

As Mr. Allingham is now about to publish a new edition of his "Spanish Armada in Ulster and Connacht," it has been considered desirable that this translation should be added to it *in extenso* for the convenience of reference. I have, therefore, gone carefully over it again, comparing it with the Spanish text, and have made some slight alterations of an occasional word or phrase in it to make the matter more explicit.

This will explain why in some of Mr. Allingham's quotations from the original translation, as given in the first edition of his paper on this subject, a word here and there may be found to differ from those contained in the present version ; but the change does not affect the sense or meaning of any passage, with, I think, a couple of exceptions.

The first of these relates to where Cuellar describes the English as going about searching "for us who had escaped [from the perils of the sea. All the monks had fled] to the woods," etc. The part within the brackets was left out in the original translation by the accidental omission of a line in copying the rough draft ; and, as the mutilated sentence still made sense, the omission was not detected at the time.

The other is the only really important change, and I will now proceed to deal with it.

The Spanish words are: " *Hacienda Norte de las montañas,*" which I originally translated as "making for the north of the mountains"; but now prefer to render by the alternative reading : " *Making for the direction of the mountains.*"

I will first show that this latter translation is also perfectly correct, and that I am justified in adopting it, and then explain my reason for doing so.

In Spanish dictionaries generally the meaning of *Norte* is given, primarily, as North, signifying either the Arctic pole, the northern part of the sphere, the polar star, the north wind, etc.; but it is also used in another and metaphorical sense.

In the best authority we have on such matters—the Dictionary of the Spanish Academy—we find that *Norte* also means *direction*, guide, "the allusion being taken from the North Star, by which navigators guide themselves with the direction of the nautical needle" [or mariner's compass]. With such an authority to support me, I think it can scarcely be disputed that the alternative translation, which I recommend, is a fair one.

I will now explain why I prefer it to my first reading of the passage. Cuellar's statement leaves no room for doubt that it was to O'Rourke's country, lying along and to the south of the Leitrim range of mountains, he was bound; while Mr. Allingham's investigations make it equally certain, in my opinion, that Glenade was the particular place Cuellar came to, as described in his account of his wanderings.

Now, as Glenade is among the Leitrim mountains, not on their northern side—along which, in the first instance, I had supposed Cuellar's route to lie—it became necessary for me to re-examine my position and make sure whether the Spanish text required a rigid adherence to my first translation, or might admit of some alternative reading that would account for the apparent discrepancy.

The result was, as already explained, that the pages of the dictionary disclosed a perfectly easy and admissible treatment of the passage in question, that solved the difficulty without the necessity of resorting to any postulates, or putting a forced or novel interpretation upon the words.

Here, perhaps, I should refer to the fact that two other translators of Cuellar's narrative—Professor O'Reilly in the *Proceedings of the Royal Irish Academy*, December, 1893, and Mr. Sedgwick in a small volume recently published by Mr. Elkin Mathews, of Vigo Street, London—give this passage a very different meaning to that which I attach to it, while they agree tolerably closely with each other.

Professor O'Reilly omits all mention of the mountains, and translates only the rest of the sentence, as: "*Taking the northerly direction pointed out by the boy*"; while Mr. Sedgwick puts it in this form: "*Striking north for the mountains* the boy had pointed out."

This latter reading gives the preposition (*de*) exactly the opposite signification to that which it usually bears.

But, apart from this, there is another and, I think, a fatal objection to the two foregoing translations of the phrase.

Both agree that the boy told Cuellar to go *straight on* to mountains, *pointed out* by him, as the place behind which O'Rourke lived. If so, these mountains could not have been situated to the north of where he was at the time, as to go from thence in anything like a northerly direction would have brought him at once into the sea, which lay to the north of him, and extended for several miles farther eastwards.

That this fact must have been apparent to both Cuellar and his guide as they went along will be recognised by those who are acquainted with the locality, which everywhere looks down upon the ocean.

There is another rather important point upon which I differ from the two gentlemen already named, who here again agree closely with each other. It relates to the position of the village in which MacClancy's retainers lived. Cuellar says it was established upon "*tierra firme*," which one translates as *firm*, the other as *solid*, ground. To me the context appears to indicate clearly that the expression was intended to bear its ordinary idiomatic interpretation of *mainland* in contradistinction to the position of the castle itself, which we are told was built in the lake.

There are several other expressions about the meaning of which we differ; but I will only refer to some of them, that are of sufficient importance, either directly or indirectly, to make it desirable that Cuellar's statement concerning them should be correctly given. I do not refer to them in any spirit of adverse criticism, but in the interests of accuracy, as regards details, in the description of an important historical event.

Both parties translate *montes* as *mountains*. This, I think, is a mistake: it should be *woods*. Cuellar repeatedly uses the correct word, *montañas*, to express mountains; so that when we find him writing *montes*, the natural inference is that he was referring to something of a different nature; besides, *montes* is frequently made use of in Spanish to denote woods.

Professor O'Reilly translates *manta* as *cloak* throughout; while Mr. Sedgwick also does so the first time he meets with it, but calls it *blanket* always afterwards. *Manta* means a blanket, but *manto* is a mantle, veil, or cloak; and the error alluded to is due, no doubt, to the similarity of the two words.

Again, both gentlemen translate *un trompeta* as a *trumpet*: it should be a *trumpeter*. The cause of the mistake here lies in overlooking the nature of the article made use of. *Trompeta* is both a masculine and feminine noun. The former signifies the man who blows a trumpet, and the latter is the instrument itself. In the present instance, the article (*un*) being masculine, shows that the word is used in its masculine sense, and therefore means a *trumpeter*.

I will now briefly refer to a few cases of the two translators separately, taking Professor O'Reilly first.

Galleon and *galley* do not translate each other, but refer to very different classes of ships.

Cuellar did not remain on board *his own ship* after he had been sentenced to death and reprieved, but was detained on the ship of the Judge Advocate, in which he was subsequently wrecked. The number of dead bodies lying on the shore where he was cast away is given by Cuellar as more than 600, not as more than 800.

"*Casiñas de paja*" means, I think, that the huts were not merely thatched with straw, but composed of it altogether. This appears to be clear from the fact that Cuellar uses another expression—"*Casas pajizas*"—when he wished to describe the thatched houses in Ocan's village.

Referring to the ship that Cuellar's companions—who outstripped him—embarked upon, and in the wreck of which they were subsequently lost, Professor O'Reilly says she "*drifted there by good luck*" (*con gran fortuna*). I think this is not the true meaning of the passage, but that the ship was driven in "*by a great tempest*" or storm; for he goes on to say that her main-mast and rigging were much injured. It should be borne in mind that *fortuna* means a storm or tempest, as well as fortune or luck.

Turning now to Mr. Sedgwick's translation, he gives *Ancients* as the English equivalent for *Alferez*, which is probably some curious misprint; for the ordinary meaning of the word is *ensign*.

Again, *Sierra* does not mean a "peak," but a mountain ridge or range.

Pelotes is given as *goat-skin*: it should be goat's *hair*.

"*Y pues el salvaje sentia tanto desmamparar su castillo*" is translated: "And since the savage had *resolved* to abandon his castle." This should be: "Besides [or since] the savage *regretted so much* to abandon his castle."

Here it may be remarked that Cuellar always calls the natives of Ireland savages, which seems very ungrateful on his part, as many of them showed him great kindness. It would have been pleasanter for a translator at the present day to have softened the harsher expression by substituting *native* for it, as Professor O'Reilly has done; but it appears to me that this does not convey the correct meaning of what Cuellar had in view when he used the word *salvaje*.

Referring to MacClancy's Castle, Cuellar says: "*Por lo qual no se puede ganar este castillo por agua, ni por la banda de tierra que esta mas cerca de el.*" Mr. Sedgwick translates it thus: "For this reason the castle is safe from attack, and is inaccessible both by water and by the strip of *land that runs up to it.*" This would look as if the castle stood upon a promontory of the mainland, instead of being built in the lake, as Cuellar, at the beginning of the same paragraph, tells us it was.

I think the true meaning of the passage is this: "For which reason the castle could not be taken by water nor by the shore of the land that is nearest to it."

To conclude: there appears to be an important error in Mr. Sedgwick's translation, beginning with the title, and repeated in the first and last sentences of this book, besides occurring several times throughout its pages. I refer to the statement that Cuellar's letter was written to King Philip II., and to the constant use of the expression "Your Majesty" to the person he was addressing.

I cannot find the slightest evidence in support of this assumption: on the contrary, everything in the letter would seem to contradict it. It is written in a familiar, chatty style, as to a person with whom the writer was on fairly familiar terms, and was certainly not such as a captain in the Spanish navy would address to his Sovereign.

The error must, I think, have arisen from some misconception as to the meaning of the abbreviations made use of in Spanish epistolary correspondence.

In twelve instances I find that Mr. Sedgwick has apparently mistaken the initials V.m. (a capital V followed by a small m), which stand for *Vuestra merced*—the usual form in which untitled persons addressed each other—for V.M. (where both letters are capitals), meaning *Vuestra Majestad* (Your Majesty). Once (on page 12) he gives a similar rendering of the letters S.M., which stand for *Su Majestad* (His Majesty), although on page 104 he translates the same initials correctly. On page 98 he uses the same formula (Your Majesty) to represent the expression *La Majestad* (The Majesty), and on page 102 he makes it do duty for the whole expression "*La Majestad del rey nuestro Señor*" (the majesty of the King, our Lord).

ROBERT CRAWFORD.

STONEWOLD, BALLYSHANNON,
March 29th, 1897.

Translation of

CAPTAIN CUELLAR'S

Narrative of the Spanish Armada.

*Letter of One who was with the Armada of [for] England,
and an Account of the Expedition.*

———————

3 BELIEVE that you [1] will be astonished at seeing this letter on account of the slight certainty that could have existed as to my being alive. That you [2] may be quite sure of this I write it [the letter], and at some length, for which there is sufficient reason in the great hardships and misfortunes I have passed through since the Armada sailed from Lisbon for England, from which our Lord, in His infinite good pleasure, delivered me.

As I have not had an opportunity to write to you [3] for more than a year, I have not done so until now that God has brought me to these States of Flanders, where I arrived twelve days ago with the Spaniards who escaped from the ships that were lost in Ireland, Scotland, and Shetland, which were more than twenty of the largest in the Armada.

In them came a great force of picked infantry, many captains, ensigns, [4] camp-masters, [5] and other war officials, besides several gentlemen and scions [6] of nobility, out of all of whom, being more than two hundred, not five survived; because some of them were drowned, and those who reached the shore by swimming were cut in pieces by the English, whom the Queen keeps quartered in the Kingdom of Ireland.

———————

(1, 2, 3). V.m., initials representing *Vuestra merced* = your worship, your honour, or sir, you.

(4). *Alférez* = ensign.

(5). *Maesos de Campo*—an obsolete form for *Maestre de Campo*, an ancient military officer of superior rank, who commanded a certain number of troops. In the English *State Papers* of that period the translation adopted for it is simply camp-master.

(6). *Mayorazgos*—heirs to estates, by right of primogeniture.

I escaped from the sea and from these enemies by having commended myself very earnestly to our Lord, and to the Most Holy Virgin, His Mother; and with me three hundred and odd soldiers, who also knew how to save themselves and to swim to shore. With them I experienced great misfortunes: naked and shoe-less all the winter: passing more than seven months among mountains and woods with savages, which they all are in those parts of Ireland where we were shipwrecked.

I think it is not right for me to omit to narrate to you, or to keep back, the injuries and the great insults [7] that it was sought to inflict upon me, so wrongfully, and without my having committed the fault of neglecting to do my duty, from which our Lord delivered me.

Having been condemned to death, as you will have known, and so ignominiously, and seeing the severity with which the order for execution was given, I demanded, with much spirit and anger, why they inflicted upon me so great an insult and dishonour, I having served the King as a good soldier and loyal subject of his on all occasions and in the encounters which we had with the fleet of the enemy, from which the galleon I commanded always came out of action very badly injured, and with many people killed and wounded.

In it (my demand) I requested that a copy of the order should be given me, and that a judicial inquiry should be made of the three hundred and fifty men who were on board the galleon, and if any one of them considered me to blame they might quarter me.

They did not wish to listen to me, nor to many gentlemen who interceded on my behalf, replying that the Duke was then in retirement, and very morose, and unwilling that any one should speak with him; because, in addition to the miserable success which he always had with the enemy, on the day of my trouble he was informed that the two galleons—*San Mateo* and *San Felipe*—of those from Portugal, in which were the two camp-masters,[8] Don Francisco de Toledo, brother of the Count of Orgaz, and Don Diego Pimentel, brother of the Marquis de Távara, were lost in the sea, and most of those they carried were cut to pieces and dead.

On this account the Duke kept to his cabin, and the councillors, to make up for his perversity, [9] did wrongs, right and left, on the lives and reputations of blameless persons; and this is so public that every one knows it.

---

(7). *Agravios* = offences, *insults*.
(8). *Maesos de Campo*. See Note 5.
(9). *Avieso* = irregular, perverse.

The galleon *San Pedro*, in which I sailed, received much injury from many heavy cannon balls, which the enemy lodged in her in various parts; and although they were repaired as well as was possible at the time, there were still some hidden shot-holes through which much water entered.

After the fierce engagement we had off Calais on the 8th of August, continuing from the morning till seven o'clock in the evening —which was the last of all—our Armada being in the act of retiring— oh! I don't know how I can say it—the fleet of our enemy followed behind to drive us from their country; and when it was accomplished, and everything was safe, which was on the 10th of the same [month], seeing that the enemy had stopped [ceased to follow], some of the ships of our Armada trimmed up and repaired their damages.

On this day, for my great sins, I was resting for a little, as for ten days I had not slept nor ceased to assist at whatever was necessary for me,—a pilot [mate], a bad man whom I had, without saying anything to me, made sail and passed out in advance of the admiral's ship for about two miles, as other ships had done, in order to effect repairs.

When about to lower sails, to see where the galleon was leaking, a tender came alongside and summoned me, on the part of the Duke, to go on board the admiral's ship. I proceeded thither; but before I reached her, orders were given in another ship that I and another gentleman, who was named Don Cristobal de Avila, who went as captain of a store-ship—which was far ahead of my galleon—should be put to death in a most ignominious manner.

When I heard of this severity, I thought I should have burst with passion, saying that all should bear me witness of the great wrong done to me, I having served so well, as could be seen by written document.

The Duke heard nothing of all this, because, as I say, he was in retirement. Señor Don Francisco Bovadilla alone was he who ordered and countermanded in the Armada; and by him, and others, whose evil deeds are well known, all was managed.

He ordered me to be taken to the ship of the Judge [10] Advocate General, that his advice should be carried out on me. I went there: and although he was severe, the Judge Advocate—Martin de Aranda, for so they called him—heard me, and obtained confidential information concerning me. He discovered that I had served His Majesty as a good soldier, for which reason he did not venture to carry out

---

(10). *Auditor* = a Judge appointed to assist military or naval officers with his advice in Law proceedings.

on me the order that had been given him. He wrote to the Duke about it, that if he did not order him in writing, and signed by his own hand, he would not execute that order, because he saw that I was not in fault, nor was there cause for it.

Accompanying it, I wrote a letter to the Duke of such a nature that it made him consider the affair carefully, and he replied to the Judge Advocate that he should not execute the order upon me, but on Don Cristobal, whom they hanged with great cruelty and ignominy, being a gentleman and well known.

God was pleased to deliver me because I was not in fault, which you will be able to know well, or will have known from many persons who saw it [eye-witnesses].

The said Judge Advocate was always very courteous to me, because of the great respect he had for those who were in the right.

I remained in his ship, in which we were in imminent danger of death, because she opened so much with a storm which sprang up that she continually filled with water, and we could not dry her out with the pumps. We had neither remedy nor succour, except it was from God; for the Duke still did not appear, and all the Armada proceeded, scattered in such manner by the storm that some ships went to Germany, others drove on the islands of Holland and Zealand into the enemies' hands, others went to Shetland, others to Scotland, where they were lost and burned. More than twenty were lost in the Kingdom of Ireland, with all the chivalry and flower of the Armada.

As I have said, the ship I sailed in was from the Levant, to which were attached two others, very large, to afford us aid if they could.

In these came Don Diego Enriquez, "the hunchback," as camp-master; and not being able to weather [round or double] Cape Clear (?), in Ireland, on account of the severe storm which arose upon the bow, he was forced to make for the land with these three ships, which, as I say, were of the largest size, and to anchor more than half a league from the shore, where we remained for four days without being able to make any provision, nor could it even be made.

On the fifth [day] there sprang up so great a storm on our beam, with a sea up to the heavens, so that the cables could not hold nor the sails serve us, and we were driven ashore with all three ships upon a beach, covered with very fine sand, shut in on one side and the other by great rocks.

Such a thing was never seen : for within the space of an hour all three ships were broken in pieces, so that there did not escape three hundred men, and more than one thousand were drowned, among them many persons of importance—captains, gentlemen, and other officials.

Don Diego Enriquez died there one of the saddest deaths that has ever been seen in the world.

In consequence of fearing the very heavy sea that was washing over the highest part of the wrecks, he took his ship's boat that was decked, and he and the son of the Count of Villa Franca and two other Portuguese gentlemen, with more than sixteen thousand ducats, in jewels and crown-pieces, placed themselves under the deck of the said boat, and gave the order to close and caulk the hatchway by which they had entered.

Thereupon more than seventy men, who had remained alive, jumped from the ship to the boat, and while she was making for the land so great a wave washed over her that she sank, and all on deck were swept away.

Then she drifted along, rolling over in different directions with the waves, until she went ashore, where she settled wrong side up, and by these mischances the gentlemen who had placed themselves under the deck died within.

More than a day and a half after she had grounded, some savages arrived, who turned her up for the purpose of extracting nails or pieces of iron; and, breaking through the deck, they drew out the dead men.

Don Diego Enriquez expired in their hands, and they stripped him, and took away the jewels and money which they (the dead men) had, casting the bodies aside without burying them.

And because it is a wonderful occurrence, and true without doubt (of a certainty), I have wished to narrate it to you in order that it may be known there (on your side) the manner in which this gentleman died.

And as it would not be right to omit to mention my own good fortune, and how I got to land, I say that I placed myself on the top of the poop of my ship, after having commended myself to God and to Our Lady, and from thence I gazed at the terrible spectacle. Many were drowning within the ships; others, casting themselves into the water, sank to the bottom without returning to the surface; others on rafts and barrels, and gentlemen on pieces of timber; others cried aloud in the ships, calling upon God; captains threw their chains and crown-pieces into the sea; the waves swept others away, washing them out of the ships.

While I was regarding this solemn [11] scene, I did not know what

---

(11). *Fiesta* = feast. This is a curious use of the word.

to do, nor what means to adopt, as I did not know how to swim, and the waves and storm were very great; and, on the other hand, the land and the shore were full of enemies, who went about jumping and dancing with delight at our misfortunes; and when any one of our people reached the beach, two hundred savages and other enemies fell upon him and stripped him of what he had on until he was left in his naked skin. Such they maltreated and wounded without pity, all of which was plainly visible from the battered ships, and it did not seem to me that there was anything good happening on any side.

I went to the Judge Advocate—God pardon him!—he was very sorrowful and depressed, and I said to him that he should make some provision for saving his life before the ship went to pieces, as she could not last for half a quarter of an hour longer; nor did she last it.

Most of her complement of men and all the captains and officers were already drowned and dead when I determined to seek means of safety for my life, and placed myself upon a piece of the ship that had been broken off, and the Judge Advocate followed me, loaded with crown-pieces, which he carried stitched up in his waistcoat and trousers.

There was no way to detach the portion of wreck from the ship's side, as it was held fast by some heavy iron chains, and the sea and the pieces of timber floating about loose struck it, nearly killing us.

I managed to find another resource, which was to take the cover of a hatchway, about as large as a good-sized table, that by chance the mercy of God brought to my hand. When I tried to place myself upon it, it sank with me to a depth of six times my height below the surface, and I swallowed so much water that I was nearly drowned.

When I came up again, I called to the Judge Advocate, and I managed to get him upon the hatchway cover with myself. In the act of casting off from the ship, there came a huge wave, breaking over us in such a manner that the Judge Advocate was unable to resist it, and the wave bore him away and drowned him, crying out and calling upon God while drowning.

I could not aid him, as the hatchway cover, being without weight at one end, began to turn over with me, and at that moment a piece of timber crushed my legs.

With great exertion, I righted myself upon my supporting timber; and, supplicating Our Lady of Ontañar, there came four waves, one after the other, and, without knowing how, or knowing how to swim, they cast me upon the shore, where I emerged, unable to stand, all covered with blood, and very much injured.

The enemies and savages, who were on the beach stripping those who had been able to reach it by swimming, did not touch me nor approach me, seeing me, as I have said, with my legs and hands and my linen trousers covered with blood. In this condition I proceeded, little by little, as I could, meeting many Spaniards stripped to the skin, without any kind of clothing whatsoever upon them, chattering with the cold, which was severe, and thus I stopped for the night in a deserted place, and was forced to lie down upon some rushes on the ground, with the great pain I suffered in my leg.

Presently a gentleman came up to me, a very nice young fellow, quite naked, and he was so dazed that he could not speak, not even to tell me who he was ; and at that time, which would be about nine o'clock at night, the wind was calm and the sea subsiding. I was then wet through to the skin,[12] dying with pain and hunger, when there came up two people—one of them armed, and the other with a large iron axe in his hands—and upon reaching me and the other [man] who was with me, we remained silent, as if we had not anything amiss [with us]. They were sorry to see us; and without speaking a word to us, cut a quantity of rushes and grass, covered us well, and then betook themselves to the shore to plunder and break open [13] money-chests and whatever they might find, at which work more than two thousand savages and Englishmen, who were stationed in garrisons near there, took part.

Managing to rest a little, I began to doze ; and when fast asleep, at about one o'clock in the night, I was disturbed by a great noise of men on horseback—there were more than two hundred of them—who were going to plunder and destroy the ships. I turned to call my companion, to see if he slept, and found he was dead, which occasioned me great affliction and grief. I got to know afterwards that he was a man of position. There he lay on the ground with more than six hundred other dead bodies which the sea cast up, and the crows and wolves[14] devoured them, without there being any one to bury them : not even poor Don Diego Enriquez.

---

(12). *Hecho una sopa de agua*—an idiomatic expression, meaning "*wet through to the skin.*"

(13). *Arca*—coffer, *iron chest for money*. The dictionary of the Spanish Academy gives a definition of *Arca*, of which the following is a translation : "A large chest, with flat lid attached to it by hinges or hooks, so that it can be opened and shut, and which is fastened in front with a lock or padlock. It usually consists of plain wood without lining in the interior or covering outside."

(14). *Wolves* did not disappear from Ireland till the early part of the eighteenth century. There was a presentment for killing them, in the County of Cork, as late as the year 1710.

At the dawn of day I began to walk, little by little, searching for a monastery of monks, that I might repair [15] to it [or might recover in it] as best I could, which I arrived at with much trouble and toil. I found it deserted, and the church and images of the saints burned and completely ruined, and twelve Spaniards hanging within the church by the act of the Lutheran English, who went about searching for us to make an end of all of us who had escaped [from the perils of the sea. All the monks had fled] to the woods [16] for fear of the enemies, who would have sacrificed them as well if they had caught them, as they were accustomed to do, leaving neither place of worship nor hermitage standing; for they had demolished them all, and made them drinking-places for cows and swine.

In order that you may occupy yourself somewhat after dinner, by way of amusement, in reading this letter, which will almost appear as if taken from some book of chivalry, I write it at such length, so that you may imagine the risks and hardships that I have experienced.

As I did not meet with any one at the said monastery, except the Spaniards hanging within from the iron window gratings of the church, I sallied forth speedily, and betook myself to a road which lay through a great wood. When I had gone by it for the matter of a mile, I met with a woman of more than eighty years of age, a rough savage, who was carrying off five or six cows to hide them in that wood, so that the English who had come to stop in her village might not take them.

As she saw me, she stopped and recognised me, and said to me : "Thou Spain." I said yes to her by signs, and that I had been ship-wrecked. She began to lament much and to weep, making me signs that I was near her house, but not to go there, as there were numerous enemies in it, and they had cut the heads off many Spaniards. All this was affliction and hardship for me, as I travelled alone, and badly injured by a stick of timber, which almost broke my legs in the water.

At last, with the information of the old woman, I decided to go to the shore, where the ships lay that were wrecked three days before, where many parties of people went about carting away and removing to their huts all our effects [spoils].

I did not venture to show myself, nor to approach them, in order that they might not strip me of the poor linen garment I had on my

(15). This might also be translated "that I might recover in it."
(16). The part within the brackets was accidentally omitted in copying the rough draft of the original translation. *Montes* signifies both mountains and woods. Cuellar uses *montaña* to signify mountain, and *montes* apparently for woods. He also makes use of *bosque*, a wood with thick underbrush, or a thicket.

back or kill me, until I saw two poor Spanish soldiers approaching, stripped naked as when they were born, crying out and calling upon God to help them.

The one bore a bad wound in the head, which they had given him when stripping him. They came to me, as I called to them from where I was concealed, and recounted to me the cruel deaths and punishments which the English had inflicted upon more than one hundred Spaniards they had taken.

With this intelligence there was no lack of affliction; but God gave me strength; and after I had commended myself to Him, and to His blessed Mother, I said to those two soldiers: "Let us proceed to the ships where these people are going about plundering, perhaps we shall find something to eat or drink, for it is certain that I shall die of hunger." And going in that direction, we began to see dead bodies, which was a great grief and pity to see those whom the sea continued casting up. There were stretched out upon that strand more than four hundred, among whom we recognised some, and the poor Don Diego Enriquez, whom, with all my sad plight, I did not wish to pass by without burying him in a pit, which we made in the sand, at the water's edge. We laid him there along with another very honourable captain, a great friend of mine, and we had not quite finished burying them, when there came up to us two hundred savages, to see what we were doing. We said to them, by signs, that we were placing there those men who were our brothers, that the crows might not eat them.

Then we went off, and searched for something to eat along the shore—of biscuits, which the sea was casting up—when four savages came up to me to strip me of the clothing which I wore, and another was grieved and took them away; seeing that, they began to maltreat me: and he may have been a chief, for they respected him.

This man, by the grace of God, assisted me and my two companions, and brought us away from there, and remained a good while in our company, until he put us on a road which led from the coast to a village where he lived. There he told us to await him, and that he would return soon and put us [17] on the way to a good place.

Along with all this misery, that road was very stony, and I was unable to move or go a step forward, because I went shoe-less, and dying with pain in one of my legs, which was severely wounded. My poor companions were naked and freezing with the cold, which was

(17). *Encaminaria* = would guide, put in the right road.

very great; and not being able to exist nor assist me, they went on in front by the road, and I remained there supplicating God's favour.

He aided me, and I began to move along, little by little, and reached a height, from whence I discovered some huts of straw;[18] and going towards them by a valley, I entered a wood.[19] When I had gone a distance of two shots of an arquebus in it, an old savage of more than seventy years came out from behind the rocks, and two young men, with their arms—one English, the other French—and a girl of the age of twenty years, most beautiful[20] in the extreme, who were all going to the shore to plunder.

When they saw me pass among the trees, they changed their course towards me, and the Englishman came up saying, "Yield, Spanish poltroon,"[21] and made a slash at me with a knife, desiring to kill me. I warded off the blow with a stick which I carried in my hand; but, in the end, he got at me, and cut the sinew of my right leg. He wanted to repeat the blow immediately, had not the savage come up with his daughter, who may have been this Englishman's friend,[22] and I replied he might do what he wished to me, for fortune had subdued me, and deprived me of my arms in the sea. They took him away from me then, and the savage began to strip me, to the taking off of my shirt, under which I wore a gold chain of the value of rather more than a thousand dollars.[23] When they saw it, they rejoiced greatly, and searched the jacket,[24] thread by thread, in which I carried forty-five crown-pieces in gold, that the Duke had ordered to be given to me at Corunna for two months' pay;[25] and when the Englishman saw that I carried a chain and crown-pieces, he wanted to take me prisoner, saying that he should be offered a ransom. I replied that I had nothing to give; that I was a very poor soldier, and had gained that, what they saw, in the ship. The girl lamented much to see the bad treatment I received, and asked them to leave me the clothes, and not to injure me any more. They all returned to the hut of the savage, and I remained among those trees, bleeding from the wound which the Englishman had inflicted upon me. I proceeded

---

(18). *Paja*—coarse grass or straw.
(19). *Bosque*—wood or thicket, with much underbrush.
(20). *Hermosisima por todo extremo.* This implies a very strong expression, consisting, as it does, of a double superlative.
(21). *Poltron* = poltroon.
(22). *Amiga* = female friend.
(23). *Real*—a Spanish coin, value a dollar.
(24). *Jubon*—doublet, jacket.
(25). *Paga*—literally means payment; but when applied to soldiers or sailors, as in this case, it means monthly pay.

to put on again my jacket and sack-coat; moreover, they had taken away my shirt, and some relics of great value which I wore in a small garment [vestment], of the Order of the Holy Trinity, that had been given to me at Lisbon.

These the savage damsel took and hung them round her neck, making me a sign that she wished to keep them, saying to me that she was a Christian : which she was in like manner as Mahomet.

From her hut they sent me a boy with a poultice made of herbs, to put upon my wound, and butter and milk and a small piece of oaten bread to eat.

I applied the dressing and ate the food, and the boy went along the road with me, showing me the direction I had to go, and advising me to avoid a village which could be seen from thence, where they had killed many Spaniards, and not one escaped that they could lay their hands upon.

He [or the person] to do me this service was born a Frenchman, who had been a soldier at Terceira, upon whom it pressed heavily to see such injury done me.

When the boy was about to turn back, he told me to continue travelling *straight towards some mountains* that appeared to be about six leagues off, behind which there were good lands belonging to an important savage very friendly to the King of Spain; and that he gave shelter to, and treated well, all the Spaniards who went to him ; and that he had in his village more than eighty of those from the ships who reached there naked.

At this news I took some courage ; and with my stick in hand, I began to walk as best I could, making for the direction of the mountains [or for the north of the mountains], as the boy had told me. [·6]

That night I reached some huts, where they did not do me harm, because there was in them one who knew Latin ; and in the necessity of the circumstances, our Lord was pleased that we should understand one another, talking Latin. I narrated to them my hardships.

The Latin-speaking man sheltered me in his hut that night: he dressed my wound, gave me supper, and a place where I might sleep upon some straw. In the middle of the night his father arrived and his brothers, loaded with plunder and our things, and it did not

---

(26). *Hacienda Norte de las montañas. Norte*, strictly speaking, means the *Arctic pole* ; but, according to the Dictionary of the Spanish Academy, it is also used, metaphorically, to mean *direction*, or guide, in allusion to the *North Star*, by which navigators guide themselves with the direction of the mariner's compass.

displease the old man that I had been sheltered in his house and well treated.

In the morning they gave me a horse and a boy to convey me over a mile of bad road that there was, with mud up to the girths. Having passed it by the distance of the shot of a cross-bow, we heard a very great noise, and the boy said to me, by signs, "Save yourself, Spain" (for so they call us); "many Sassana horsemen are coming this way, and they will make bits of thee if thou doest not hide thyself; come this way quickly." They call the English "Sassanas." He took me away to hide in some rugged places among the rocks, where we were very well concealed. They would be about one hundred and fifty horsemen going back to the coast to plunder as many Spaniards as they found.

God delivered me from them; and, proceeding on our way, there fell in with me more than forty savages on foot, and they wished to make little pieces of me because they were all Lutherans. They did not do it, as the boy, who came with me, told them that his master had taken me prisoner, and he had me in custody, and had sent me on that horse to be cured. With all this, it did not suffice to obtain permission for me to pass in peace; for two of those robbers came up to me and gave me six blows of a stick, which bruised my shoulders and arms, and they stripped me of everything that I wore, so as to leave me as naked as when I was born. I speak the truth, by the holy baptism which I received. And seeing myself in this condition, I gave many thanks to God, beseeching of His Divine Majesty that He would fulfil His will on me, as that was what I desired.

The boy of the savage wished to return to his hut with his horse, weeping to see how I was left, stripped naked, so badly treated, and so cold.

I begged of God, very earnestly, that He would transport me to where I should die confessed and in His grace. I took some courage, being in the greatest extremity of misfortune that man ever saw, and with some bracken leaves and a small piece of old matting which I wrapped around my body, I protected myself from the cold as best I could.

I continued travelling, little by little, towards the place that had been pointed out to me, searching for the territory of the chief who had protected the Spaniards; and, reaching the mountain range that they gave me for direction, I met with a lake, around which there were about thirty huts, all forsaken and unoccupied, and there I wished to pass the night.

Not having where to go, I sought out the best hut, which appeared to me best to take shelter in for the night; and, as I say, they were unoccupied and without people. On entering the door, I saw it was full of sheaves of oats, which is the ordinary bread that those savages eat, and I gave thanks to God that I was so well off as to have a place to sleep on them; but just then I saw three men emerge from one side, naked as when their mothers had brought them forth, and they stood up and stared at me. They gave me a fright, for I thought they were, without doubt, devils, and they understood no less that I might be so, swathed in my ferns and matting. As I entered, they did not speak to me, because they were quaking, nor, any more, did I to them, not having observed them, the hut being somewhat dark. Seeing myself in this great perplexity, I said: "Oh! Mother of God, be with me, and deliver me from all evil."

When they saw [? heard] me speaking Spanish, and calling upon the Mother of God, they also said: "Let that great Lady be with us."

Then I felt reassured, and went up to them, asking them if they were Spaniards.

Yes, we are, for our sins, they replied. Eleven of us were stripped together at the shore, and in this naked state we came to seek some land of Christians. On the way, there met us a party of enemies, who killed eight of us, and the three who are here made our escape through a wood so thick that they could not discover us. That evening, God provided us with these huts, where we have rested, though there are no people in them nor anything to eat.

I said to them, then, to be of good courage, and to commend themselves always to our Lord; that near to where we were there was a land of friends and Christians; and that I brought word of a village, which was three or four leagues distant, that belonged to Señor de Ruerque [O'Rourke], where they had sheltered many of our lost Spaniards; and, although I was very badly treated and wounded, on the morrow we should proceed thither.

The poor fellows rejoiced, and they asked me who I was. I told them I was Captain Cuellar. They could not believe it, because they had felt sure I was drowned; and they came up to me, and almost completely killed me with embraces.

One of them was an ensign, and the other two private soldiers. And as the narrative is ludicrous, and true, as I am a Christian, I must proceed to the end with it, in order that you may have something to laugh at.

I got into the straw, well buried in it, with care, not to injure nor disturb its position ; and, having arranged to rise in the morning for our journey, we slept without supping, not having eaten anything but blackberries and water-cresses.

And when, in God's good time, day broke, I was wide awake with the great pain I felt in my legs, I heard talking and the noise of people ; and at this juncture there came to the door a savage, with a halberd in his hand, and he began to look at his oats and to talk to himself.

I remained without breathing, and my companions, who had been aroused, [were] watching the savage very attentively from under the straw, and what he intended to do.

It was the will of God that he went out and left, with many others who had come along with him, to reap and work close to the huts in a place where we could not go out without being seen. We remained quiet, buried alive, discussing what it would suit us to do, and we decided not to disinter ourselves, nor to move from that place while those heretic [27] savages were there, who were from the place where so much evil was done to the poor fellows of our Spaniards whom they caught ; and they would have done the same to us if they had perceived us there, where we had no one to protect us but God.

Thus passed the whole day ; and then, when night came on, the traitors departed to shelter themselves at their villages, while we awaited the rising of the moon.

Then wrapped up with straw and hay, for it was extremely cold, we sallied forth from that great danger, in which we had been, without waiting for the day.

We went along, stumbling in the mud, and dying with hunger, thirst, and pain, until God was pleased to bring us to a land of some safety, where we found huts of better people, although all savages, but Christians and charitable. One of them, seeing that I came so badly treated and wounded, took me to his hut and dressed my wounds, he and his wife and sons, and he did not permit me to depart till it appeared I should be well able to reach the village I was bound for. In it I met with more than seventy Spaniards, who all went about naked and severely maltreated, because the chief was not there.

He had gone to defend a territory which the English were coming to take ; and although this man is a savage, he is a very good Christian and an enemy of heretics, always carrying on war with them. He is called Señor de Ruerque [O'Rourke].

I arrived at his house with great exertion, enveloped in straw and

---

(27). *Aquellos herejes salvajes*—literally, heretics, savages, both being nouns.

swathed around the body with a piece of matting, in such a plight that no one could see me without being moved to great compassion.

Some of the savages gave me a bad old blanket, full of vermin, with which I covered myself, and somewhat improved matters.

Early next day, about twenty of us Spaniards collected together at the house of this Señor de Ruerque [O'Rourke], in order that they might give us something to eat, for the love of God; and while we were there begging, news was told us that a Spanish ship was at the coast, that she was very large, and came for those Spaniards who had escaped.

With this news, without waiting longer, the whole twenty of us left for the direction where they told us the ship was, and we met with many hindrances on the way; though, for me it was an advantage and a mercy which God granted me that I did not arrive at the port where she was in the same manner as the others who were with me reached it. They embarked on board of her, as she belonged to the Armada, and had arrived there in a great gale [28] with her main-mast and rigging much injured. Fearing that the enemy might burn her or do her some other injury, for which energetic preparations were being made, they set sail from thence in two days with the crew that came in her and those they had picked up, returning, to run aground and get wrecked, on the same coast. More than two hundred persons were drowned, and those who reached the shore by swimming were taken by the English and all put to death. [29] It pleased God that I alone remained of the twenty who went in search of her, for I did not suffer like the others. For ever blessed be His Most Holy Pity for so great mercies as He has shown to me.

Going along thus, lost with much uncertainty and toil, I met by chance with a road along which a clergyman in secular clothing was travelling (for the priests go about thus in that kingdom, so that the English may not recognise them). He was sorry for me, and spoke to me in Latin, asking me to what nation I belonged and about the ship-wrecks that had taken place. God gave me grace so that I was able to reply to everything he asked me in the same Latin tongue; and so satisfied was he with me, that he gave me to eat of that which he carried with him, and he directed me by the right road that I should

---

(28). *Fortuna*—generally means *fortune* or *chance*, but it also signifies a *storm* or *tempest*. It is in this latter sense that it appears to be used here; for Cuellar goes on to describe the injured state in which the ship was.

(29). *Y los pasaron todos á cuchillo* = and they passed them all to the *knife*. An idiomatic expression in Spanish corresponding to the English one, *were put to the sword*.

go to reach a castle, which was six leagues from there. It was very strong, and belonged to a savage gentleman, a very brave soldier and great enemy of the Queen of England and of her affairs, a man who had never cared to obey her or pay tribute, attending only to his castle and mountains, which made it strong.

I set out for there, experiencing much trouble on the road, and the greatest, and that which gave me most pain, was that a savage met me on the way, and, by deceiving me, took me to his hut in a deserted valley, where he said I must live all my life, and he would teach me his trade, which was that of a blacksmith. .

I did not know what to answer nor did I venture,[30] so that he should not put me in the forge. Before him I showed a pleasant countenance, and proceeded to work with my bellows for more than eight days, which pleased the wicked savage blacksmith, because I did it carefully, so as not to vex him and an accursed old woman he had for wife.

I was in tribulation and sad with such miserable employment, when our Lord favoured me by causing the clergyman to return by that way, who was surprised to see me, because that savage did not wish to let me go away, as he made use of me. The clergyman scolded him severely, and told me not to be troubled, as he would speak with the chief of the castle to which he had directed me, and get him to send for me, which he did the following day. He sent four men of the savages, who served him, and a Spanish soldier, of whom he had already ten with him of those who had escaped by swimming.

When he saw me so stripped [of clothing] and covered with straw, he and all those who were with him grieved greatly, and their women even wept to see me so badly treated.

They helped me as best they could with a blanket of the kind they use, and I remained there three months, acting as a real savage like themselves.

The wife of my master was very[31] beautiful in the extreme, and showed [did] me much kindness. One day we were sitting in the sun with some of her female friends and relatives, and they asked me about Spanish matters and of other parts, and in the end it came to be suggested that I should examine their hands and tell them their fortunes. Giving thanks to God that it had not gone even worse with

<hr />

(30). Cuellar has not expressed himself clearly here, but he seems to mean that he did not oppose the blacksmith's wishes.

(31). *Muy hermosa por todo extremo.* This is a slight modification of a similar expression on a previous occasion. See Note 20.

me than to be gipsy among the savages, I began to look at the hands
of each, and to say to them a hundred thousand absurdities, which
pleased them so much that there was no other Spaniard better than I,
or that was in greater favour with them.

By night and by day men and women persecuted me to tell them
their fortunes, so that I saw myself (continually) in such a large crowd
that I was forced to beg permission of my master to go from his castle.
He did not wish to give it me : however, he gave orders that no one
should annoy me or give me trouble.

The custom of these savages is to live as the brute beasts among
the mountains, which are very rugged in that part of Ireland where
we lost ourselves. They live in huts made of straw. The men are
all large bodied, and of handsome features and limbs ; and as active
as the roe-deer.[32] They do not eat oftener than once a day, and
this is at night ; and that which they usually eat is butter with oaten
bread. They drink sour milk, for they have no other drink ; they
don't drink water, although it is the best in the world. On feast days
they eat some flesh half-cooked, without bread or salt, as that is their
custom. They clothe themselves, according to their habit, with tight
trousers [33] and short loose coats [34] of very coarse goat's hair.[35] They
cover themselves with blankets, [36] and wear their hair down to their
eyes. They are great walkers, and inured to toil. They carry on
perpetual war with the English, who here keep garrison for the Queen,
from whom they defend themselves, and do not let them enter their
territory, which is subject to inundation, and marshy. That district
extends for more than forty leagues in length and breadth. The
chief inclination of these people is to be robbers, and to plunder each
other ; so that no day passes without a call to arms among them. For
the people in one village becoming aware that in another there are
cattle, or other effects, they immediately come armed in the night,
and "go [37] Santiago" [attack], and kill one another ; and the English
from the garrisons, getting to know who had taken, and robbed, most
cattle, then come down upon them, and carry away the plunder.
They have, therefore, no other remedy but to withdraw themselves to
the mountains, with their women and cattle ; for they possess no other

(32). *Corzos* = roe-deer. *Cervus capreolus,* or *Capreolus caprea.*
(33). *Calzas* = trousers, hose.
(34). *Sayos* = loose coats.
(35). *Pelotes* = goat's hair.
(36). *Mantas* = blankets.
(37). *Anda Santiago.* This is a slang expression, meaning to attack. It is
derived from the fact that *Santiago* was the war-cry or watchword of the Spaniards
when going into action, *Santiago* being the patron saint of Spain.

property, nor more moveables nor clothing. They sleep upon the ground, on rushes, newly cut and full of water and ice.

The most of the women are very beautiful, but badly [38] dressed [got up]. They do not wear more than a chemise, and a blanket, with which they cover themselves, and a linen cloth, much doubled, over the head, and tied in front. They are great workers and housekeepers, after their fashion. These people call themselves Christains. Mass is said among them, and regulated according to the orders of the Church of Rome. The great majority of their churches, monasteries, and hermitages, have been demolished by the, hands of the English, who are in garrison, and of those natives who have joined them, and are as bad as they. In short, in this kingdom their is neither justice nor right, and everyone does what he pleases.

As to ourselves, these savages liked us well because they knew we came against [to oppose] the heretics, and were such great enemies of theirs; and if it had not been for those who guarded us as their own persons, not one of us would have been left alive. We had good-will to them for this, although they were the first to rob us and strip to the skin those who came alive to land; from whom, and from the thirteen ships of our Armada, in which came so many people of importance, all of whom were drowned, these savages obtained much riches in jewellery and money.

Word of this reached the great Governor of the Queen, who was in the city of Dililin [Dublin], and he went immediately, with seventeen hundred soldiers, to search for the lost ships and the people who had escaped. They were not much fewer than one thousand men, who, without arms and naked, were wandering about the country in the locality where each ship had been lost.

The majority of these the Governor caught, and hanged them at once or inflicted other penalties, and the people who he knew had sheltered them he put in prison, and did them all the injury he could.

In this manner he took three or four savage chiefs, who had castles, in which they had sheltered some Spaniards; and, having put both parties under arrest, marched with them along the whole of the coasts till he arrived at the place where I was wrecked. From thence he turned off towards the castle of Manglana [MacClancy], for so they called the savage with whom I was, who was always a great enemy of the Queen, and never loved anything of hers, nor cared to obey her, for which reason he (the Governor) was very anxious to take him prisoner.

---

(38). *Compuestas* = composed, made up.

This savage, taking into consideration the great force that was coming against him, and that he could not resist it, decided to fly to the mountains, which was his only remedy : more he could not do.

We Spaniards, who were with him, had news of the misfortune which was coming upon us, and we did not know what to do, or where to place ourselves in safety.

One Sunday, after mass, the chief, with dishevelled hair down to his eyes, took us apart, and, burning with rage, said that he could not remain, and he had decided to fly with all his villagers, their cattle, and their families, and that we should settle what we wished to do to save our lives. I replied to him to calm himself a little, and that presently we would give him an answer. I went apart with the eight Spaniards who were with me—they were good fellows—and I told them they should well consider all our past misfortunes and that which was coming upon us; and in order not to see ourselves in more, it was better to make an end of it at once honourably ; and as we had then a good opportunity, we should not wait any longer, nor wander about flying to the mountains and woods, naked and barefooted, with such great cold as there was. Besides, the savage regretted so much to abandon his castle, we, the nine Spaniards who were there, would cheerfully remain in it and defend it to the death. This we could do very well, although there should come two other such forces, more than that which was coming, because the castle is very strong and very difficult to take if they do not (even though they should) attack it with artillery ; for it is founded in a lake of very deep water, which is more than a league wide at some parts, and three or four leagues long, and has an outlet to the sea ; and, besides, with the rise of spring tides it is not possible to enter it, for which reason the castle could not be taken by water nor by the shore of the land that is nearest to it. Neither could injury be done it, because [for] a league round the town, which is established on the mainland, it is marshy, breast-deep, so that even the inhabitants [natives] could not get to it except by paths.

Then, considering all this carefully, we decided to say to the savage that we wished to hold the castle and defend it to the death ; that he should, with much speed, lay in provisions for six months, and some arms.

The chief was so pleased with this, and to see our courage, that he did not delay much to make all provision, with the concurrence [good-will] of the principal men of his town, who were all satisfied. And, to insure that we should not act falsely, he made us swear that we would not abandon his castle, nor surrender it to the enemy for any bargain or agreement, even if we should perish from hunger; and not to open the gates for Irishman, Spaniard, or any one else till his return, which he would doubtless accomplish.

Then, all that was necessary being well prepared, we moved into the castle, with the ornaments and requisites for the Church service, and some relics which were there, and we placed three or four boat-loads of stones within, and six muskets, with six cross-bows, and other arms. Then the chief, embracing us, retired to the mountains, all his people having already gone there; and the report was spread throughout the country that Manglana's [MacClancy's] Castle was put in a state of defence, and would not be surrendered to the enemy, because a Spanish captain, with other Spaniards who were within, guarded [held] it.

Our courage seemed good to the whole country, and the enemy was very indignant at it, and came upon the castle with his forces—about eighteen hundred men—and observed us from a distance of a mile and a half from it, without being able to approach closer on account of the water which [39] intervened. From thence he exhibited some warnings, and hanged two Spaniards, and did other damages [injuries] to put us in fear. He demanded many times, by a trumpeter, [40] that we should surrender the castle, and he would spare our lives and give us a pass to Spain. We said to him that he should come closer to the tower, as we did not understand him, appearing always to make little of his threats and promises [words].

We had been besieged for seventeen days, when our Lord saw fit to succour and deliver us from that enemy by severe storms and great falls of snow, which took place to such an extent that he [the Queen's Governor] was compelled to depart with his force, and to march back to Duplin [Dublin], where he had his residence and garrisons. From thence he sent us warning that we should keep ourselves out of his hands, and not come within his power; and that he would return in good time to that country.

We replied to him much to our satisfaction, and to that of our Governor of the castle, who, when he got the news that the English-men had retired, returned to his town and castle greatly appeased and calmed, and they *féted* us much.

He [the chief] very earnestly confirmed us [admitted us to full

---

(39). *Por el agua que habia de por medio.*

(40). *Un trompeta* = a trumpeter. This noun is both *feminine* and *masculine*, meaning, respectively, *a trumpet* and *a trumpeter*. The masculine article *un* shows that the noun is used here in its masculine form.

privileges] as most loyal friends : offering whatever was his for our service, and the chief persons of the land [did the same], neither more nor less. To me he would give a sister of his, that I should marry her. I thanked him much for this ; but contented myself with a guide to direct me to a place where I could meet with embarkation for Scotland.

He did not wish to give me permission [to leave], nor to any Spaniard of those who were with him, saying that the roads were not safe ; but his sole object was to detain us, that we might act as his guard.

So much friendship did not appear good to me ; and thus I decided, secretly, with four of the soldiers who were in my company, to depart one morning two hours before dawn, so that they should not pursue [? stop] us on the road : and also because one day previously a boy of Manglana's [MacClancy's] had told me his father had said that he would not let me leave his castle until the King of Spain should send soldiers to that country ; and that he wished to put me in prison, so that I might not go.

Possessed of this information, I dressed myself as best I could, and took to the road, with the four soldiers, one morning ten days after the Nativity, [41] in the year 88.

I travelled [went travelling] by the mountains and desolate places, enduring much hardship, as God knows : and at the end of twenty days' journey, I got to the place where Alonzo de Leyva, and the Count de Paredes and Don Tomas de Granvela, were lost, with many other gentlemen, to give an account of whom would need a quire [42] of paper.

I went to the huts of some savages that were there, who told me of the great misfortunes of our people who were drowned at that place, and showed me many jewels and valuables of theirs, which distressed me greatly.

My chief cause of misery was that I had no means of embarking for the Kingdom of Scotland ; until one day I heard of the territory of a savage, whom they called Prince Ocan, where there were some vessels that were going to Scotland. Thither I travelled, crawling along, for I could [scarcely] move because of a wound in one leg ; but, as it led to safety, I did all I could to walk, and reached it quickly. The vessels had left two days before, which was no small disappointment for me, as I was in a very dreadful country and among enemies,

---

(41). *Christmas.*
(42). *Mano de papel* = a quire of paper.

there being many English stationed at the port, and each day they were with Ocan.

At this time I suffered great pain in the leg, so much so that in no manner could I stand upon it. I was advised, too, that I should be very cautious, because there were many English there who would do me great harm if they caught me, as they had done to other Spaniards; especially if they knew who I was.

I did not know what to do, as the soldiers who came with me had left, and gone to another port further on to seek for a passage.

Some women, when they saw me alone, and ill, pitied me, and took me away to their little huts on the mountain, and kept me there for more than a month and a half in safety, and cured me, so that my wound healed, and I felt well enough to go to Ocan's village to speak with him.

But he did not wish to hear or see me; for, it was said, he had given his word to the great Governor of the Queen not to keep any Spaniard in his territory, nor permit one to go about in it.

The English, who were quartered there, having marched off to invade a territory and take it, Ocan accompanied them with all his force, so that one could go openly [boldly] about the village, which was composed of thatched huts.

In them there were some very beautiful girls, with whom I was very friendly, and went into their houses occasionally for society and conversation.

One afternoon, while I was there, two young Englishmen came in, one of whom was a sergeant, and possessed information of me, by name, but yet had not seen me before. When they were seated, they asked me if I were a Spaniard; and what I was doing there. I said yes; that I was one of the soldiers of Don Alonzo de Luçon, who had lately surrendered to them; but on account of a bad leg, I had not been able to leave the district; that I was at their service, to do whatever they wished to command.

They told me to wait a little, and that I should have to go with them to the city of Dublin, where there were many important Spaniards in prison.

I said that I could not walk or go with them, and they sent to search for a horse to carry me. I told them I was very willing to do whatever they wished, and to go with them, with which they were reassured, and began to make fun with the girls.

Their mother made signs to me to go away (that I should leave by the door), and I did so in great haste, leaping banks as I went along. I got among thick brambles, into which I penetrated until I lost sight of Ocan's Castle, following this course until I wished to lie down for the night.

I had arrived at a very large laguna [lake or marsh], along the banks of which I saw a herd of cows walking, and I was approaching to see if there was any one with them who could tell me where I was, when I observed two boy savages advancing. They came to collect their cows, and take them up the mountain to where they and their fathers were hiding for fear of the English ; and there I spent two days with them, being treated with much kindness.

One of the boys had to go to the village of the Prince of Ocan to ascertain what news or rumour there was, and he saw the two English-men, who were going about, raging, in search of me.

Information about me had already been given to them, and no one passed by whom they did not ask if he had seen me.

The boy was such a good lad that, upon learning this, he returned to his hut, and informed me of what had occurred, so that I had to leave there very early in the morning, and to go in search of a bishop, who was seven leagues off in a castle where the English kept him in banishment and retirement. This bishop was a very good Christian, and went about in the garb of a savage for concealment, and I assure you I could not restrain tears when I approached him to kiss his hand. He had twelve Spaniards with him for the purpose of passing them over to Scotland, and he was much delighted at my arrival, all the more so when the soldiers told him that I was a captain. He treated me with every kindness [43] that he could for the six days I was with him, and gave orders that a boat should come to take us over to Scotland, which is usually done in two days. He gave us provisions for the voyage and said mass to us in the castle, and spoke with me about some things concerning the loss of the kingdom, and how His Majesty had assisted them ; and that he should come to Spain as soon as possible after my arrival in Scotland, where he advised me to live with much patience, as in general they were all Lutherans and very few Catholics. The bishop was called Don Reimundo Termi (?) [? Bishop of Times], an honourable and just man. God keep him in His hands and preserve him from his enemies.

That same day at dawn [44] [when it was growing light], I went to

(43). Cuellar uses the word *courtesy* on several occasions where *kindness* is what he seems to mean.

(44). Mass appears to have been said in the night-time, and the preparations may also have been made during the night, so that the boat might leave at daylight, and not attract too much attention.

sea in a wretched boat in which we sailed 18 persons—and the wind becoming contrary the same day, we were forced to run before it, at the mercy of God, for Shetland, where we reached the land at daylight ; the boat being nearly swamped, and the main-sail carried away. We went on shore to give thanks to God for the mercies He had bestowed upon us in bringing us there alive ; and from thence, in two days, with good weather, we left for Scotland, where we arrived in three days : not without danger, on account of the great quantity of water the miserable boat took in.

We blessed God who withdrew us from such perils and so great hardships, and brought us to a land where there might be more succour.

It was said that the King of Scotland protected all the Spaniards who reached his kingdom, clothed them, and gave them passages to Spain ; but all was the reverse, for he did no good to anyone, nor did he bestow one dollar in charity. Those of us who reached that kingdom suffered the greatest privations ; inasmuch, as we were [left] for more than six months as naked as when we arrived from Ireland, and other places, to seek succour and assistance there, and passages to Spain.

I am inclined to believe that he was much persuaded, on the part of the Queen of England, to hand us over to her. And had not the Catholic Lords and Counts of that kingdom helped us—and there were many, and great gentlemen, to favour us and speak for us to the King, and in the Councils which were held on the subject—without doubt we should have been betrayed [sold], and handed over to the English. For the King of Scotland is nobody : nor does he possess the authority or position of a king : and he does not move a step, nor eat a mouthful, that is not by order of the Queen. Thus, there are great dissensions among the gentlemen, who bear him no good-will, and desire to see his reign ended, and the Majesty of the King, our Lord, in his place, that he might establish the Church of God, which has been brought to such ruin there.

This they said to us many times, almost weeping, longing to see that day which, they hoped in God, might soon arrive.

And, as I say, these gentlemen supported us all the time that we were there, and gave us much alms, and were kind to us, sorrowing for our misfortunes, with much pity. They asked us to have patience, and to bear with a people who called us idolaters and bad Christians, and said a thousand heresies to us ; for, if one made answer, they would fall upon him and kill him, and it was impossible to live or

remain in such a bad kingdom with so bad a king. . . . . .*
A despatch was sent to the Duke of Parma . . . .* at which
his Highness, as a pious prince, grieved, and with great zeal he sought
to succour us . . . .* to the King, that he would permit us to
leave his kingdom, and to the Catholics and friends much gratitude
on the part of his Majesty, with his most friendly letters.

There was a Scotch merchant in Flanders, who offered and agreed
with his Highness that he would come to Scotland for us and ship us
in four vessels, with the provisions which were necessary, and that he
would bring us to Flanders, his Highness giving him five ducats for
each Spaniard of those that he brought to Flanders.

The agreement was made with him, and he went for us and
embarked us, unarmed and naked as he found us, and took us by the
ports of the Queen of England, which secured us permission to pass
by all the fleets and ships of her kingdom.

All was treacherous ; for an arrangement had been made with the
ships of Holland and Zealand that they should put to sea and await
us at the same bar [entrance to the harbour] of Dunkirk, and there
they should put us all to death, without sparing one, which the Dutch
did as they were commanded ; and were on the look-out for us for a
month and a half at the said port of Dunkirk, and there they should
have caught us all had not God helped us.

God willed that of the four vessels in which we came, two escaped
and grounded, where they went to pieces ; and the enemy, seeing the
means of safety which we were taking, gave us a good discharge of
artillery, so that we were forced to cast ourselves afloat [45] [to make a
desperate attempt], and we thought to end it there.

They could not come to our assistance with the boats from the
port of Dunkirk, as the enemy cannonaded them briskly. On the
other hand, the sea and wind were very high ; so that we were in the
greatest peril of being all lost.

However, we cast ourselves afloat [46] on timbers, and some soldiers
were drowned, as was also a Scotch captain. I reached the shore in
my shirt, without other description of clothing, and some soldiers of
Medina (?) who were there came to help me.

It was sad to see us enter the town once more, stripped naked ;

---

* Here the manuscript is stated to be torn and illegible.
(45). *Echarnos a nado. Echarse a nado* literally means to cast oneself afloat ;
but it has also a metaphorical signification—viz., *to make a desperate attempt.* As
the same expression is made use of twice close together, it may be that in the first
instance it was meant metaphorically ; but this is by no means certain.
(46). See preceding Note.

and for the other part we saw, as before our eyes, the Dutch making a thousand pieces of two hundred and seventy Spaniards who came in the ship which brought us to Dunkirk, without leaving more than three alive ; for which they are now being paid out, as more than four hundred Dutchmen who have been taken since then have been beheaded. This I have wished to write to you.

From the City of Antwerp, 4th October, 1589.

Sgd.

FRANCISCO DE CUELLAR.

ACADEMY OF HISTORY—COLLECTION SALAZAR,
No. 7, FOLIO 58.

INDEX.

ILLUSTRATIONS.

www.ingramcontent.com/pod-product-compliance
Lightning Source LLC
Chambersburg PA
CBHW030026030726
47499CB00008B/3135